USING AI FOR BEGINNERS

A SIMPLE GUIDE TO AUTOMATE REPETITIVE TASKS, SAVE TIME, AND BOOST PRODUCTIVITY IN LESS THAN A WEEK

WESLEY THOMAS

CONTENTS

Introduction 7

1. UNDERSTANDING AI BASICS 11
Defining Artificial Intelligence 12
Understanding Machine Learning 13
Machine Learning Example: Spam Email Detection 14
The Evolution of AI 15
Demystifying Artificial Intelligence 16
Key AI Terms: What You Need to Know 18
Machine Learning vs. Deep Learning: A Simple Breakdown 20
How AI is Changing Everyday Life 21

2. SETTING UP FOR AI SUCCESS 25
Creating an AI-Friendly Digital Workspace 25
Upgrading Hardware and Software 26
Leveraging Productivity Tools 26
Ensuring Cybersecurity 27
Building a Supportive Learning Environment 28
The Role of Peer Support 28
Set Achievable Goals 29
Optimize Your Learning Experience 29
Essential Tools for AI Beginners 30
Choosing the Right AI Tools for Your Needs 31
Integrating AI with Your Existing Technology 31

3. OVERCOMING AI LEARNING BARRIERS 35
Tackling the Fear of AI Complexity 35
Learning AI with Limited Time 38
Affordable AI: Free Tools You Can Use 40
Finding Reliable AI Resources 42

4. AUTOMATING DAILY TASKS IN 7 DAYS 47
Day 1: Automate Email Sorting with AI 47
Day 2: Simplifying Calendar Management Automatically 49
Day 3: Streamlining Social Media with AI Bots 51
Day 4: AI-Powered Financial Management 53
Day 5: Use AI to Edit Correspondence and Documents 54
Day 6: Create Content Using AI 56
Day 7: Ponder the Ethics and Implications of AI Use 57

5. PERSONAL PRODUCTIVITY BOOSTS WITH AI 61
AI for Personal Task Management 61
Enhancing Personal Creativity with AI Tools 63
Using AI for Efficient Time Management 65
AI Solutions for Personal Organization 67

6. AI IN PROFESSIONAL SETTINGS 73
Automating Project Management Tasks 73
Enhancing Workplace Communication with AI 76
Successful Data Analysis Case Studies 78
AI-Driven Decision Making 79

7. CREATIVE APPLICATIONS OF AI 84
Designing with AI: From Canva to Midjourney 84
Writing Assistance with Tools Like Grammarly 87
AI-Powered Art with DALL-E 89
AI in Music and Video Creation 91

8. DATA PRIVACY AND ETHICS IN AI 95
Understanding AI's Ethical Implications 95
Safeguarding Your Data When Using AI 99
Responsible AI Practices 102
Balancing AI Benefits with Ethical Concerns 105

9. INTERACTIVE AI LEARNING 110
Test Your Knowledge With AI Quizzes 110
Hands-On Exercises for Practical AI Skills 114

Real-World AI Challenges: Can You Solve Them? 117
Building Confidence: Small Wins with AI 119

10. REWIND: REAL-WORLD AI SUCCESS STORIES 124
Groundbreaking AI in Healthcare 124
Case Study—Fetal Monitoring By AI 125
Case Study—AI-Assisted Robotic Surgery 126
AI Innovations in Retail and E-commerce 127
AI's Role in Modern Education 129
AI in Finance: Case Studies and Outcomes 131
AI in Creative Industries 134
AI in Transportation and Logistics 135
AI in Environmental Conservation 136

11. MORE ADVANCED AI TOOLS FOR BEGINNERS 138
Exploring Advanced Interactions Using ChatGPT 138
Ideogram and Creative AI Outputs 141
Scribbr for Enhanced Writing and Editing 143
Reedsy: Publishing with AI Assistance 144
Keeping Up with AI Trends 145
Continuous Learning and AI Skill Development 147
Join AI Communities for Support 148

12. PERSONALIZED AI JOURNEYS 152
Crafting Your Unique AI Learning Path 152
Personalized AI Learning Tools. 156

Conclusion 161
References 165
Glossary of AI Terms 171
AI Tools Referenced in This Book 175

INTRODUCTION

Eight years back, I found myself drowning in a sea of emails and repetitive tasks. That Tuesday afternoon, routine tasks swamped me as I sat staring at my laptop screen. I decided then and there to find a way out. Enter AI. My first encounter with AI was a revelation. I stumbled upon a simple AI tool that promised to sort my emails and handle my scheduling. Skeptical but desperate, I gave it a shot. By the end of the week, I realized I had gained back hours of my work week. My productivity soared, and I felt renewed control over my work and my schedule.

This is the promise of AI—a promise that is increasingly becoming a reality for people across the globe. AI is now a reality. Businesses are using AI to optimize operations, educators are leveraging it to enhance learning experiences, and individuals are finding new ways to improve their productivity. A recent report suggested that AI will boost business productivity by up to 40% by 2035. This is more than a trend; it's a transformation.

The book's purpose is straightforward, yet impactful. It's to make AI accessible to everyone, especially beginners who feel intimidated by the tech-heavy jargon. You won't need a coding background or expensive software. You will need a willingness to explore and commit to applying what you learn. In less than a week, you will automate repetitive tasks, saving precious time, and boosting your productivity. To help get you started, I include a glossary of AI terms and a list of accessible AI tools at the back of this book.

The book's structure guides you step by step. We'll start with the basics, laying establishing what AI is and how it works. As you progress through the chapters, you'll discover practical applications tailored to real-world scenarios. Key chapters will walk you through setting up AI tools, automating mundane tasks, and even exploring creative uses of AI in design and writing.

Allow me to introduce myself. I'm Wesley Thomas, and I have spent over 30 years in the telecommunications and technology sectors. My journey has seen me champion innovation and drive technology adoption both as an employee of Fortune 500 companies and as a consultant to companies of all shapes and sizes. For 20 years, I taught college courses, helping students and professionals grasp emerging technologies. Today, I run my consulting firm, showing businesses and individuals how AI can be a game-changer.

One of the biggest misconceptions about AI is that it's only for tech experts or requires costly software. This couldn't be further from the truth. AI is for everyone. It's about making life easier, not complicated. Throughout this book, we'll tackle these myths head-on, showing you how to leverage AI without breaking the bank or needing a computer science degree.

So, what can you expect from this book? By the end, you'll have newfound confidence in using AI tools. You'll learn practical skills for automating tasks that drain your energy and time. You'll find inspiration for integrating AI into your personal and professional life. This is not just about learning; it's about transforming how you work and live. Furthermore, failure to use AI tools puts you at risk of falling behind in your profession.

I encourage you to approach this book with openness and curiosity. Dive into the exercises and examples. Experiment. The more you engage, the more you'll gain. AI is a tool that can unlock potential you didn't know you had. However, like any tool, AI is only productive when used by a competent user.

As we transition into the main content, prepare to explore a world where technology serves you, not the other way around. Together, we'll take practical steps to harness AI's power, transforming how you approach work and life. Welcome to a journey of discovery and empowerment. Let's get started.

1
UNDERSTANDING AI BASICS

"Machine intelligence is the last invention that humanity will ever need to make."

— NICK BOSTROM

I fondly remember sitting in a coffee shop sipping coffee and using the free Wi-Fi when a conversation captured my attention and set off a proverbial light bulb in my mind. Two young professionals sitting at the table behind me were animatedly discussing the transformative power of AI and its impact on their productivity. Their palpable enthusiasm was contagious; I found myself leaning back in my chair to listen, captivated by a desire to learn more. This epiphany made me realize the extent to which AI has subtly infiltrated our daily lives, often without overtly making its presence felt. This chapter aims to simplify AI for you, making it as familiar and comprehensible as your routine morning cup of coffee.

DEFINING ARTIFICIAL INTELLIGENCE

Artificial Intelligence, abbreviated as AI, is a captivating segment of computer science committed to crafting machines that demonstrate human-like intelligence. These machines handle tasks necessitating problem-solving skills, language comprehension, pattern recognition, and the ability to learn from experiences. Unlike the broad spectrum of human intelligence, AI typically falls into two categories: narrow and general. Narrow AI shines in specific domains and targeted use cases, such as recommending Netflix shows or correcting grammar with Grammarly. General AI represents a loftier goal that machines could learn to perform any intellectual task a human can perform. This aspiration remains on the horizon of technological development, yet it draws closer with each fresh development.

AI's history is a narrative celebrating human innovation and relentless pursuit. It traces back to pioneers like Alan Turing, who dared to ask, "Can machines think?" His groundbreaking speculations set the stage for what has evolved into a dynamic field. From early conversational programs like Eliza to IBM's Deep Blue besting chess master Garry Kasparov, AI's journey is marked by significant milestones. Today's advancements in natural language processing and image recognition exemplify AI's expanding capabilities, driven by tremendous data volumes and leaps in computational power.

In today's fast-paced world, AI is omnipresent—from virtual assistants like Siri and Alexa to chatbots improving customer service interactions. Big data's role in AI development is crucial; it is the powerhouse behind intelligent systems. As you delve into AI's numerous applications in every facet of life, remember that this book prioritizes practical applications over speculative theories. Whether you are automating your daily regimen or engaging in innovative AI-driven projects, the emphasis is on making AI accessible and applicable to your regular activities.

UNDERSTANDING MACHINE LEARNING

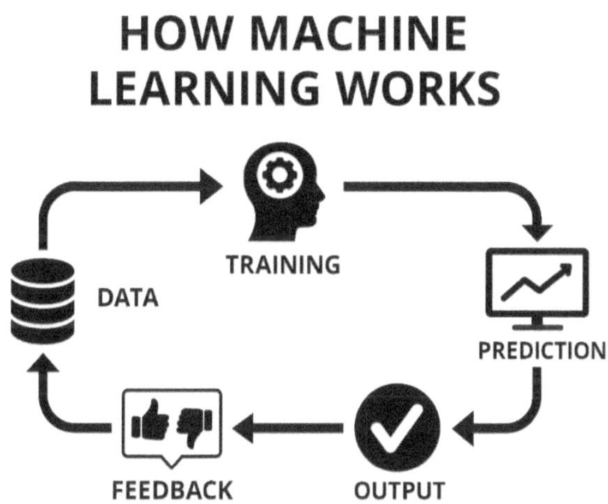

Machine learning, commonly referred to as ML, delves into an engaging subset of artificial intelligence focused on empowering machines to learn and make informed decisions from available data. You could liken it to teaching your computer, allowing it to derive insights from experiences akin to human learning. The crux of this learning process is data. Consider teaching a child to differentiate fruits by showing them dozens of examples until they discern apples from oranges. Similarly, ML models depend heavily on extensive datasets to develop patterns and predictions.

Two key types of machine learning are prevalent: supervised learning and unsupervised learning. Supervised learning trains models using labeled datasets; each example in these datasets is paired with its expected output. For instance, envision your email's spam filter, which learns to differentiate between spam and genuine emails through user examples. Unsupervised learning operates without labeled data, akin to asking a machine to categorize a box of assorted items based on inherent similarities. Unsupervised learning is prevalent in clustering tasks, where it is particularly helpful.

When discussing machine learning, it's pivotal to grasp key algorithms that underlie AI applications. Linear regression helps explain relationships between variables, such as predicting real estate prices based on location and square footage. Decision trees are another standard algorithm for classification tasks like identifying spam emails. As mentioned, clustering involves categorizing data into coherent groups based on shared attributes.

MACHINE LEARNING EXAMPLE: SPAM EMAIL DETECTION

How does your computer's spam detector know which messages are spam? The answer is machine learning. Your mail client learns as it looks at thousands of emails that people have marked as "spam" and "not spam." The email program finds patterns by noticing common traits in spam emails—like words such as "free money," excessive punctuation (!!!), or suspicious links. Based on its knowledge about spam messages, the program then uses those patterns to predict whether it's spam—*without being programmed to recognize every spam word.*

Machine learning also allows AI tools to grow smarter over time. As you mark an email as spam (or not spam), the system learns from your feedback and adjusts its predictions. Machine learning happens as the computer learns from ongoing examples and thus improves its decisions over time—just like a human would after reading hundreds of emails.

The significance of data in ML is immense. High-quality data serves as the catalyst, igniting the potential of machine learning models. Clean, labeled datasets are fundamental for deriving accurate forecasts and insights. During the training phase, models learn from these datasets, finding patterns and correlations. Extensive testing ensures reliability when models process new, unseen data. The quality and volume of data directly influence a model's success, underscoring the need for robust datasets to enable effective machine learning.

THE EVOLUTION OF AI

AI's origins trace back to the mid-20th century, a period marked by a burgeoning interest in computing technologies. During this era, Alan Turing posed his seminal question, "Can machines think?"—a query that spurred a revolution and led to the creation of the Turing Test, a measure of how capable a machine intelligence is at mimicking humans to the extent one cannot distinguish the AI action from a human action. The 1950s and 60s witnessed symbolic AI's emergence, aiming to mimic human reasoning through symbolic representation. Landmark programs like Logic Theorist and General Problem Solver set foundational milestones for future innovation. As the 1980s and 90s unfolded, AI underwent a renaissance with machine learning's rise, heralding a shift from programmed systems to those learning from data. This period saw IBM's Deep Blue achieve fame by defeating Garry Kasparov in chess. Today, we are in the age of deep learning, where neural networks emulate the intricacies of the human brain.

Recent breakthroughs have cemented AI's position in mainstream industries. AlphaGo's triumph over human Go champions signifies AI's capability to master complex tasks that were once the sole domain of human intellect. Progress in natural language processing has introduced tools like GPT-3 and Siri, capable of comprehending and responding to human language with astonishing accuracy. At the same time, computer vision has advanced, endowing machines with the ability to interpret visual information akin to human perception. These developments are driven by the vast proliferation of big data and powerful computing resources, fueling AI's continuous growth.

AI's depiction in movies and television has profoundly affected public perception. Films like "The Matrix" and "Ex Machina" explore AI's potential and pitfalls, often portraying it as a double-edged sword. While these narratives captivate audiences, they also contribute to misconceptions about AI's realities. Nonetheless, AI continues to pervade society, impacting everything from healthcare to entertainment.

AI's potential is boundless. Quantum computing stands as a future frontier with the promise of augmenting processing capabilities exponentially, paving the way for unimaginable breakthroughs. Autonomous vehicles present another promising horizon, with AI set to revolutionize transportation by ushering in an era of self-driving automobiles. As these technologies evolve, they will reshape industries and redefine our interactions with machines in unprecedented ways.

DEMYSTIFYING ARTIFICIAL INTELLIGENCE

Artificial Intelligence, often enveloped in mystique, fundamentally revolves around simulating human intelligence in machines. It empowers computers to undertake tasks once considered unique to humans, such as problem-solving, learning, and language comprehension. AI primarily aims to automate these processes, boosting decision-making efficiency and speed. It's crucial to clarify that AI isn't about supplanting humans; instead, it complements our abilities. Envision AI as an adept assistant managing recurring and data intensive tasks, allowing humans to concentrate on what genuinely demands human insight.

At its essence, AI functions through algorithms—the precise, methodical instructions steering a machine's operations. These algorithms serve as the backbone of the AI machine, while data provides essential fuel. Imagine data as the copious information fed into systems, which guides AI in learning and adapting. Processing more data makes AI more intelligent and capable. While this may seem complex at first, AI's ease of accessibility has grown remarkably. Today, user-friendly platforms empower anyone to engage with AI, even without a technical background. Devices like smartphones and smart home gadgets exemplify AI in action, seamlessly intertwining into our daily lives.

Misunderstandings often lead to depictions of AI as futuristic or even perilous. In reality, AI's capabilities today are centered on augmenting rather than replacing human tasks. The notion of an AI takeover remains embedded in the realm of speculative fiction. Ethical development is essential to ensure AI systems are designed with human well-being at their core. As we advance further into the realm of AI, it becomes increasingly important to recognize that its role must be limited to enhancing human capabilities, not replacing them.

With accessible tools within reach, AI transcends the exclusive domain of tech devotees. Platforms such as Canva and Grammarly exemplify how AI is able to simplify creative tasks like design and writing, illustrating its newfound accessibility for everyone. Understanding AI's purpose and learning its components will dispel myths and unveil its true potential. As we move forward, it is imperative that we limit AI's role to assistance, not intimidation.

KEY AI TERMS: WHAT YOU NEED TO KNOW

Artificial Intelligence, or *AI*, signifies a revolutionary concept within technology. It denotes machines' ability to execute tasks associated with human intelligence, such as learning, solving problems, and interpreting natural language. *Machine Learning (ML)* is a subset of AI that teaches computers to learn from data sources without explicit programming intervention. *Deep Learning*, another pivotal subset, employs *neural networks* —complex algorithms inspired by human cognition—to tackle sophisticated tasks like image recognition. Familiarity with these terms is fundamental as they are at the core of AI applications, making their understanding crucial for comprehending AI tools' functionality in real-world scenarios.

Algorithms are AI's cornerstone, providing sequential instructions that drive machines to resolve issues. Think of them as recipes guiding a chef through the culinary process. Central to ML is data-driven decision-making, involving data analysis for crafting insightful predictions or decisions. Netflix's recommendation system exemplifies this approach; it uses algorithms to suggest content based on viewing history. Systems like Siri and Alexa use AI to understand and respond to spoken commands, highlighting AI's practical application in daily technology.

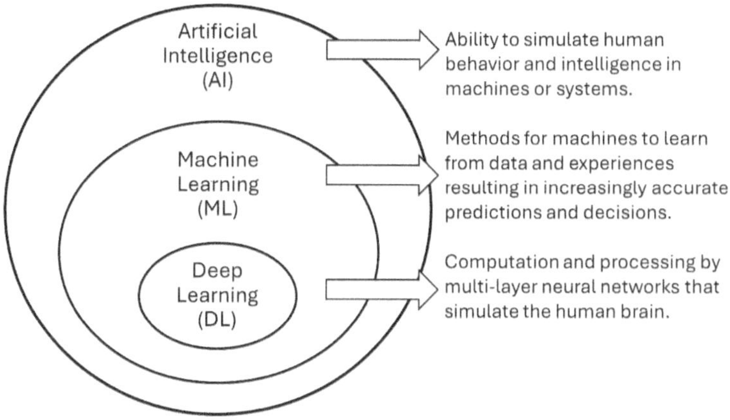

Visualize a glossary serving as your quick-reference manual for these terms. For instance, AI denotes machine intelligence; ML represents its data learning capabilities; Deep Learning highlights using neural networks for sophisticated tasks. *Algorithms* are guided directions for these processes.

Familiarity with when and how to use these terms bolsters your comprehension of their respective roles across diverse contexts. Whether discussing AI's role in predictive analytics or automation in customer service, these terms provide clarity and precision.

Consider that when you inquire about the weather, Alexa responds instantly. That's AI at work, interpreting your voice and instantly retrieving data to deliver a prompt answer. Consider Netflix, which refines its suggestions based on your viewing history—that's Machine Learning harnessing algorithms to predict your preferences. These everyday instances reflect AI's seamless integration into our lives, making familiarity with these terms both practical and empowering.

MACHINE LEARNING VS. DEEP LEARNING: A SIMPLE BREAKDOWN

Machine Learning and Deep Learning constitute the backbone of contemporary artificial intelligence, each having distinct roles despite being closely interconnected. Machine Learning is the overarching term for systems learning from provided data and data from ongoing experiences to make decisions. Deep Learning, on the other hand, is a nuanced branch of Machine Learning characterized by using neural networks that mirror the human brain's structure. These networks empower machines to tackle complex tasks, such as recognizing faces in images or executing real-time language translation. While both rely heavily on data, Deep Learning requires access to substantial datasets to train these complex networks effectively.

Illustrative examples highlight this distinction. Email filtering is a classic Machine Learning task where algorithms sift through emails, categorizing them as spam or legitimate mail. This straightforward process uses labeled data for informed decisions. Conversely, Deep Learning tackles more complex challenges like image and speech recognition. Whether using voice assistants to understand spoken commands or apps to identify objects in photos, you are witnessing Deep Learning's capabilities. These applications demand that the AI system grasp nuances and context, making sophisticated neural networks indispensable.

Data is the cornerstone for both Machine Learning and Deep Learning, although in different ways. Machine Learning thrives on quality—clean, well-labeled datasets ensure precise outcomes. Deep Learning, however, demands both data quality and quantity. Extensive datasets are essential for training neural networks to recognize patterns and make accurate predictions. For example, an AI language interpreter must understand the words being spoken and how different voice inflections can change the meaning of those words. This Deep Learning application requires data sets of both word definitions and audio files to function correctly. This data reliance underscores the importance of meticulous data preparation and labeling in both domains.

AI technologies promise groundbreaking possibilities and breakthroughs. Deep Learning's potential in autonomous systems will enable widespread use of self-driving vehicles and ever improving medical care. Machine Learning continues to evolve, with emerging developments honing optimization and efficiency. These advancements promise to redefine industries, altering how we engage with daily technology. As AI technologies steadily advance, grasping these distinctions is vital for anyone aiming to leverage AI's capabilities.

HOW AI IS CHANGING EVERYDAY LIFE

Envision waking up to the aroma of freshly brewed coffee, lights gradually illuminating, and the thermostat adjusting to your ideal temperature—all orchestrated by AI in smart home devices. These gadgets adapt to your routines, rendering daily activities seamless and efficient. AI also permeates areas beyond personal comfort. It revolutionizes personal finance apps, transforming how we manage money. These applications scrutinize spending habits, propose budgets, and offer insightful investment advice, aiding in effortless financial goal attainment. Such technology empowers us to make informed choices, preserving both time and resources.

Beyond personal convenience, AI is revolutionizing entire industries. In healthcare, AI bolsters diagnostic accuracy and tailors treatments for individuals. By expeditiously analyzing medical data, AI uncovers patterns that elude even seasoned professionals. This analysis leads to early disease detection and personalized treatment plans, dramatically elevating patient outcomes. Retail also experiences transformation through AI-powered customer service and inventory management systems. Virtual assistants adeptly manage queries, while algorithms predict stock requisites, minimizing waste and enhancing customer satisfaction.

Within the professional sphere, AI enhances productivity by automating mundane tasks, leaving us free to concentrate on creative and strategic initiatives. Scheduling assistants manage meetings, prioritize responsibilities, and send reminders, streamlining workflows. Automation oversees routine office chores like data entry, liberating employees to engage in meaningful endeavors. This results in a more motivated workforce and enhanced business outcomes.

We must consider the ethical implications of AI in every endeavor it impacts. Responsible AI development is paramount, requiring transparent practices and prioritizing human rights. Society must engage in serious, reasoned dialogue about these issues, harmonizing innovation with ethical responsibility. For example, how do we ensure privacy and security when machines manage sensitive data? Acceptance of AI must include acknowledging its formidable power and our responsibility to guide its evolution prudently.

The pervasive influence of AI is undeniable. Artificial intelligence is rapidly transforming nearly every aspect of modern life. It enhances efficiency in our homes and drives innovation across entire industries. Yet, as AI becomes more powerful, it is essential to examine its broader effects on society carefully and comprehensively.

Chapter 1 Reader Quiz

Quizzes serve as both an enjoyable and insightful method to assess your comprehension. Let's evaluate how much you have grasped about AI with these questions. Consider this an opportunity to reinforce your learning while pinpointing areas for further exploration.

1. **Which of the following is a subset of Artificial Intelligence?**

A) Robotics, B) Deep Learning, C) Quantum Computing, or D) Virtual Reality

2. **What is the primary function of machine learning?**

A) To mimic human emotions, B) To learn from data without explicit programming, C) To perform tasks with pre-set algorithms only, or D) To generate random data sets

3. **Which type of AI is specifically designed to perform a single task?**

A) General AI, B) Narrow AI, C) Super AI, or D) Meta AI

4. **What is a typical application of AI in everyday life?**

A) Predicting weather patterns with 100% accuracy, B) Automating personal finances with budgeting apps, C) Replacing all human jobs with robots, or D) Creating virtual worlds for video games only

5. **Why is data crucial in AI systems?**

A. It adds aesthetic value to AI systems, B) It allows AI systems to make informed decisions and improve over time, C) It is used once and then discarded, or D) It makes AI systems costly and inefficient

Answers:

1-B, 2-B, 3-B, 4-B, 5-B

Reflect on your responses and revisit any sections that proved challenging. Developing a deeper understanding of AI's complexities will strengthen your ability to apply its capabilities professionally and in everyday life. As you continue exploring this dynamic field, remember that each insight contributes to a solid foundation for real-world use. Stay curious, think critically, and embrace the journey of continuous learning.

2
SETTING UP FOR AI SUCCESS

"AI is the new electricity."

— AI PIONEER
ANDREW NG

CREATING AN AI-FRIENDLY DIGITAL WORKSPACE

I recall vividly the life-altering moment I decided to streamline my digital chaos into a more structured AI-friendly environment. Initially, my desktop resembled a digital dumping ground, swamped with an assortment of files. This disarray was an anchor, dragging productivity down and causing a lag in system performance due to outdated software clutter. The realization struck that to engage with AI fully, I needed a space that fostered efficiency. Visualize your digital workspace as the cockpit of a high-tech aircraft—it needs to be sleek, organized, and optimized for operation. Begin by systematically organizing your files—create intuitive folder structures with descriptive labels reflecting the content. Categorize them by project, task type, or importance to make information retrieval as seamless as possible. Regular maintenance is key; periodically evaluate your files. Delete or transfer obsolete files to an external drive or cloud storage. This routine saves space and enhances data retrieval efficiency.

UPGRADING HARDWARE AND SOFTWARE

Your hardware and software must be upgraded to meet the minimum requirements of AI applications. This is non-negotiable. Your device's ability to run AI applications involves more than just software updates. It's about maximizing your machine's performance, which often requires boosting your RAM or transitioning to Solid State Drives (SSDs) to improve processing speed. Consider the impact of a lag-free experience. Tasks that once took hours can be completed in minutes, providing more time for innovation and exploration. These hardware optimizations are pivotal in maintaining a workspace conducive to current AI tool requirements, preventing system bottlenecks, and fostering an environment ripe for innovation.

LEVERAGING PRODUCTIVITY TOOLS

Incorporating productivity tools that complement AI can radically transform your workflow. Trello's visual project management system lets you break tasks into manageable stages, providing oversight and insight into project progression. Its board features can transform how teams manage assignments and deadlines, leading to smoother project execution. Meanwhile, Evernote acts as a digital extension of your thought processes, capturing ideas, notes, and inspiration in a cohesive and comprehensive manner. Its compatibility with numerous platforms makes it an invaluable tool for maintaining an organized digital life.

ENSURING CYBERSECURITY

Security remains paramount amidst these advancements. Just as you wouldn't leave your home unlocked, your digital domain demands robust security measures. Utilize strong, unique passwords and change them periodically. Software updates are crucial for closing potential security vulnerabilities; neglecting them can expose your system to cyber threats. Installing reliable antivirus software is another defense layer, safeguarding your data against malicious attacks. Protecting your workspace ensures that your AI tools and data remain secure, reducing the risk of breaches and data losses. As you integrate AI more deeply into your daily routines, treat cybersecurity not as a secondary concern, but as an integral component of your digital strategy.

Interactive Element: Set Up Your Workspace Checklist

- Organize files into logical and intuitive folders.
- Confirm that your hardware can support AI applications.
- Ensure all software is updated to avoid compatibility issues.
- Protect your system with strong antivirus solutions.
- Leverage productivity aids such as Trello and Evernote.

This checklist serves as a roadmap, guiding you toward establishing a digital space that is efficient and ready to leverage AI technology's full potential. By embracing these changes, you set the stage for enhanced productivity and security in your AI exploration.

BUILDING A SUPPORTIVE LEARNING ENVIRONMENT

In my journey into AI, the community I found proved invaluable. Community engagement goes beyond mere learning; it's about belonging to a dynamic circle of continuous dialogue and feedback. Online forums and chat groups are dynamic hotbeds of innovation and collaboration, teeming with individuals with similar interests and challenges. These discussions allow for a richer learning experience, turning what once felt like isolated study hours into vibrant exchanges full of energy and insight. Participating in webinars or virtual meetups opens additional avenues for networking and gathering diverse perspectives, enriching your understanding of AI's multifaceted nature. These platforms foster intellectual growth, letting you tap into global insights and broaden your horizons.

THE ROLE OF PEER SUPPORT

Peer support acts as a catalyst for motivation and experimentation. Much like a dedicated study partner, peers provide encouragement and fresh viewpoints. Collaborative group projects enhance learning through practical application and promote the exchange of ideas, fostering an environment of mutual growth and discovery. Consider the power of diverse perspectives: each team member brings unique knowledge and skills, paving the way for innovative solutions. Participation in study groups or collaboration with others to explore AI concepts transforms learning from a solitary task into an interactive, engaging pursuit. The camaraderie and shared wisdom you gain from these interactions are invaluable, propelling your understanding beyond theoretical knowledge.

SET ACHIEVABLE GOALS

Maintaining motivation requires setting distinct, achievable goals. Divide your learning journey into smaller, manageable tasks and celebrate the milestones you achieve. These small wins—mastering a new algorithm or completing a hands-on project—boost morale and sustain progress. Cultivating motivation isn't about constant enthusiasm, but involves regular nurturing through intentional actions and reflection. By reflecting on your progress, you bolster your motivation to tackle more extensive and complex AI challenges.

OPTIMIZE YOUR LEARNING EXPERIENCE

Clear learning objectives are the cornerstone of effective AI education. Define what you want to achieve in the short term, like understanding a new programming language, alongside long-term aspirations like applying AI in your professional endeavors. Aligning these goals with personal and professional aspirations maintains focus and motivation as you witness AI's real-world applications unfold in your career trajectory.

World-class education platforms like Coursera and edX feature courses designed to fit diverse skill levels, offering a structured approach that guides you from foundational concepts to advanced techniques. Complement these resources with dynamic content from AI-focused podcasts and blogs, informing you of the latest developments and insights in the field. Consider subscribing to AI-driven newsletters or engaging with influencers on platforms like LinkedIn and

Twitter to stay abreast of industry trends. This blend of structured learning and ongoing updates creates a holistic educational experience.

ESSENTIAL TOOLS FOR AI BEGINNERS

Your AI journey is easier when you start with user-friendly tools. Platforms like Canva, Grammarly, and ChatGPT offer intuitive interfaces, breaking down complex tasks into simple steps. Canva's drag-and-drop features deliver eye-catching visuals without prior design expertise. Grammarly offers real-time feedback, enhancing your writing with ease and clarity. Meanwhile, ChatGPT acts as a conversational assistant, offering inspiration and answers in an engaging, accessible manner. Together, these tools embody the democratization of AI, making sophisticated capabilities accessible to all.

The accessibility and affordability of these tools are notable advantages. With free tiers available, tools like Canva, Grammarly, and ChatGPT invite experimentation without financial burden. Canva's free plan includes ample design features to spark creativity, Grammarly offers basic tools in its free version, and ChatGPT provides complimentary fundamental interactions. These free versions allow for exploratory learning and innovation without economic constraints, making them ideal entry points into AI's vast potential.

Integration capabilities add tremendous value by seamlessly fitting these tools into existing workflows. Canva can sync with Google Workspace, enabling effortless collaboration on design projects. Grammarly integrates with Microsoft Office, offering seamless writing help directly in your documents. ChatGPT aids in drafting emails or brainstorming ideas on the fly. These integrations make AI tools a seamless extension of current routines, enhancing efficiency without requiring significant adjustments.

CHOOSING THE RIGHT AI TOOLS FOR YOUR NEEDS

Choosing the right AI tools starts with a clear vision of what you want to achieve. Specific goals—like boosting customer engagement or streamlining your study routine—will point you toward the tools that truly fit. A focused list of tasks you'd like to automate or improve can sharpen your direction and lead you straight to the solutions that matter most. Be careful at this stage to avoid advertisements hiding as informational sources by checking sources.

Access to free or trial versions allow you to evaluate AI tools before committing to paying for a license. Consider a test run; explore the capabilities, ease of use, and compatibility to find the ideal AI solution tailored to your needs. During these evaluations, prioritize user-friendliness and the availability of support services, as these significantly impact your experience with the tool. This thorough approach ensures you choose tools that best suit your objectives, setting the stage for success.

INTEGRATING AI WITH YOUR EXISTING TECHNOLOGY

AI tools should augment your present setup, not impede it. Imagine seamlessly syncing an AI scheduling assistant with your calendar app—suddenly managing your appointments becomes precise and effortless, eliminating double bookings and saving time. This level of integration needs real-time data synchronization between AI tools and current software. This connectivity ensures that modifications in one application are instantly reflected across all platforms, maintaining consistency and reducing clutter. It's like adding a modern component to a classic engine, enhancing functionality without losing familiarity.

Examples of successful AI integration abound. The use of AI-driven analytics within Excel transforms raw data into insightful visual reports that empower faster, informed decision-making. An AI scheduling assistant further automates calendar management, significantly reducing errors and time investment. These illustrations show that AI is not a substitute, but a powerful enhancer of current capabilities, amplifying what your existing tools can accomplish. Consider AI an ally that extends the reach of your current technological arsenal, optimizing efficiency and refining outcomes.

Many advantages are gained by adding AI to your tech stack. It boosts the performance of existing technologies, streamlines operations, and reallocates resources to more strategic tasks. By automating repetitive tasks and delivering deeper data insights, AI enables innovative work strategies and creates productivity-boosting interaction between old and new technology. Rather than causing disruption, AI serves as a driving force for progress—enhancing every aspect of your technology efforts.

Chapter 2 Reader Quiz

As you navigate the complexities of AI, taking a moment to assess your comprehension is crucial. This quiz aims to reinforce your knowledge, not test for perfection. Engage with a series of true or false statements to solidify what you have learned:

1. **True or False:** A well-structured learning plan can enhance AI learning outcomes by breaking complex topics into manageable sections.
2. **True or False:** Peer support is less valuable in AI learning than personal study.
3. **True or False:** AI tools like flashcard apps can make learning more efficient.
4. **True or False:** Free or trial versions of AI tools are not effective for beginners because they lack features.
5. **True or False:** Regularly updating your software is unnecessary when maintaining a secure digital environment.

Answers:

1-True, 2-False, 3-True, 4-False, 5-False

Reflect on your responses and revisit any areas that sparked uncertainty. Each step fortifies your foundation, increasing your confidence and proficiency as you incorporate AI into your everyday life.

As we conclude Chapter 2, remember that setting up for AI success involves more than just tools and technology. It's about nurturing a supportive environment, optimizing your learning strategy, and selecting the right resources to facilitate a smooth journey. These foundational elements prepare you for the practical applications we'll explore in the following chapters. We'll delve deeper into hands-on automation techniques, applying your newfound insights to achieve tangible results. Let us continue to embrace AI's potential, fostering growth and development in both personal and professional spheres.

3
OVERCOMING AI LEARNING BARRIERS

> *"Artificial intelligence is not a substitute for human intelligence; it is a tool to amplify human creativity and ingenuity."*
>
> — FEI-FEI LI, FORMER CHIEF SCIENTIST OF AI/ML AT GOOGLE CLOUD, CO-FOUNDER OF WORLD LABS

TACKLING THE FEAR OF AI COMPLEXITY

I once sat across from a friend who visibly recoiled at the mere mention of artificial intelligence. Her eyes widened in apprehension as she confessed, "AI just sounds too complicated for me." This sentiment is more prevalent than one might think. Many perceive AI as daunting, envisioning a maze of complex algorithms and unfathomable code. But here's the catch: AI isn't as intimidating as it seems. You can conquer that fear by deconstructing these intricate concepts into bite-sized, manageable pieces. This book is your guide to simplifying those complexities and is designed to make AI as approachable as your favorite smartphone app.

Start with small, manageable tasks. Don't plunge headlong into crafting a machine learning model. Instead, begin with something simple, like using an AI tool to organize your daily schedule or help draft an email. Each victory builds confidence, demonstrating that you can integrate AI into your routine without a PhD in computer science. With each step, your understanding deepens, and the fear of complexity dissipates.

One can liken building confidence in AI to learning a new language. At first, it feels alien, filled with unfamiliar terms and concepts. But with time and practice, it becomes second nature. Embrace a growth mindset and understand that mistakes are part of the AI learning process. Every error is a step towards mastering AI. Patience and perseverance are crucial. Remember, even seasoned AI experts started as novices. Fortunately, several learning platforms offer interactive tools that simulate real-life scenarios, allowing you to experiment in a risk-free environment. This type of engagement provides profound insights into how AI operates in practical applications, further reducing apprehension by demystifying its intricacies.

User-friendly AI tools are game changers. They democratize access to technology that was once confined to computer labs and tech giants. Take a tool like Notion, which uses AI to make organizing thoughts, projects, and plans intuitive for the user. Notion allows you to integrate text, visuals, and databases into a single document, facilitating creative yet structured workflows. Its AI-driven suggestions serve as an intelligent assistant that adapts to your unique working style. In a similar manner, Grammarly uses AI to correct errors and refine sentence structure, offering real-time insights into writing techniques that enhance overall communication skills. This book's structure mirrors this simplicity, guiding you through each concept.

Facing challenges can drain motivation, but setting achievable goals reignites your drive. Celebrate each milestone, no matter how small—setting up an AI task manager or mastering a new feature are both accomplishments! Supportive communities also boost motivation. Online forums and local meetups offer encouragement and shared learning, reminding you're not alone. For example, AI enthusiast groups on Reddit provide inspiration and practical tips from fellow learners. Webinars and workshops offer insights, networking, and connections with experts eager to share their knowledge.

User Activity: Reflect on Previous Success

Think of a recent learning experience where you felt intimidated but overcame your fear through perseverance and practice. What strategies did you use to build confidence? How can you apply these strategies to learning AI? Write down your thoughts and revisit them whenever you feel discouraged. Consider creating a personal journal to document your AI learning progress, which will motivate you when you look back at how far you have come.

AI is more than just technology; it's an opportunity to enhance your life in meaningful ways. As you navigate this chapter, remember that fear of complexity is natural, but surmountable. By breaking down barriers and embracing each step forward, you are not only learning AI, but expanding your capabilities and horizons. Embrace the journey as an adventure filled with discovery and growth.

LEARNING AI WITH LIMITED TIME

Finding time to learn AI may feel like trying to squeeze an elephant into a suitcase. You are juggling work, family, and perhaps even school, so adding AI into the mix seems difficult, but it is possible. It is important to recognize these time constraints so you can set up strategies to make AI learning efficient. Start by using short bursts of focused study sessions rather than long marathons. Psychological research shows that breaking learning into small, manageable chunks increases understanding and retention. It's like snacking on knowledge instead of gorging. Incremental learning enhances memory retention, unlike cramming sessions, which usually lead to quick burnout.

Flexibility is your ally. Adapt your learning to fit your schedule, not the other way around. You likely have a few minutes during your morning commute or while waiting for an appointment. Use these moments to dive into bite-sized AI lessons. Online platforms, such as Google's AI courses, offer perfect modules for such occasions, allowing you to learn at your own pace. This flexible approach ensures that even the busiest schedule can accommodate quality AI learning.

A personalized learning plan can revolutionize your approach to AI learning. Begin by setting clear, realistic goals. What do you want to achieve? Is it understanding basic AI concepts or applying AI in your job? Prioritize these topics based on what matters most to you. Once you have this clarity, set up a weekly schedule with dedicated time slots for learning. Treat these slots as sacred appointments with your future self. Consistency, even in small doses, leads to considerable progress.

Time management tools are invaluable for learners. Applications like Trello or Asana can help organize your study schedule by dividing tasks into achievable steps. They act as digital planners, reminding you of what's next on your learning agenda. AI-driven time-tracking tools can optimize study sessions by analyzing where you spend the most time and suggesting improvements. These insights help refine your approach, allowing you to focus on what enhances your learning experience. For instance, platforms like RescueTime offer insights into your daily habits, highlighting time losses and providing suggestions to increase productivity. AI apps incorporating Pomodoro techniques divide study time into structured intervals, helping maintain focus and reduce mental fatigue.

Maximizing limited learning time requires planning. Focused sessions with specific objectives ensure that every minute counts. Instead of vague goals like "learn AI," aim for targeted outcomes such as "understand neural networks" or "apply AI in marketing." Micro-learning techniques further support this by offering quick, digestible lessons on complex topics. These methods keep you engaged and prevent information overload. Aim to integrate practical exercises within these sessions, as applying theoretical knowledge in real-world scenarios enhances comprehension and retention.

Interactive Element: Time Audit Exercise

Track your daily activities for a week to identify periods where you can fit in AI learning. Look for gaps in your schedule, such as lunch breaks or evening downtime, and allocate short study sessions during these times. This exercise helps uncover hidden opportunities for productive learning. In addition to discovering hidden time pockets, evaluate and adjust your routine to eliminate low-value activities, reallocating those minutes to AI learning to further boost efficiency.

An efficient plan that is tailored to your life is key. With dedication and the right tools, you can integrate AI learning seamlessly into your day-to-day routine without feeling overwhelmed or sacrificing other commitments. By strategically planning and utilizing available resources, you'll find that learning AI is possible and rewarding, even within a hectic schedule. Embrace the learning journey as an enriching experience, aligning it with your personal and professional development goals.

AFFORDABLE AI: FREE TOOLS YOU CAN USE

In the vast world of AI, cost needn't be a barrier. Many believe that delving into AI necessitates a hefty investment, but that's far from true. Numerous practical tools are available for free or at minimal cost. These resources offer robust capabilities without demanding a cent upfront. For beginners, this is excellent news. You can explore AI's potential without financial strain. Tools like Google's TensorFlow and OpenAI's GPT-3 offer free tiers that provide ample features for learning and experimentation. Canva and Grammarly also have freemium models, allowing you to access essential features at no cost while offering premium options for advanced capabilities. These platforms are designed for accessibility, making them perfect starting points for anyone new to AI.

If you know where to look, accessing these resources is straightforward. Start by exploring open-source platforms, which offer a wealth of free tools and software. Websites like GitHub and Kaggle are treasure troves of open-source projects where you can find AI applications tailored to various needs.

Even better, many online courses and tutorials are available at no cost. Websites like Coursera and edX often offer free access to their course materials if you are not seeking a certificate. This allows you to learn from top institutions without paying hefty tuition fees. Also, initiatives like Mozilla's common voice project encourage contributions to free datasets, enriching the learning pool for everyone.

Free AI tools offer more than budget-friendliness; they are gateways to skill-building. These tools grant access to high-quality features typically reserved for expensive software, allowing you to develop your skills without the pressure of financial risk. You can experiment, make mistakes, and learn without worrying about subscription costs piling up. The ability to engage with these technologies without economic barriers means that anyone with curiosity and determination can enhance their knowledge, regardless of their financial situation.

Consider the stories of those who've harnessed the power of free AI solutions to achieve remarkable outcomes. Take, for example, a student who used free design software like Canva to create stunning presentations for school projects, impressing both peers and teachers with professional-grade visuals. Or a small business owner who tapped into free AI tools to automate customer engagement, enhancing service quality without inflating costs. These real-world examples highlight how accessible AI tools can transform tasks into opportunities for innovation and efficiency. Similarly, educators are incorporating these tools into the classroom, fostering a new generation adept in AI through interactive projects and collaborative learning experiences.

Reader's Resource: AI Resource List

- **TensorFlow**: Open-source platform for machine learning.
- **Kaggle**: Community for data science projects and competitions.
- **Google AI Courses**: Free educational resources for beginners.
- **Canva**: A Freemium design tool with AI capabilities.
- **Grammarly**: Writing assistant with free tier features.

These resources are stepping stones into the expansive world of AI, offering hands-on experience at no cost. They present an opportunity to explore, learn, and grow your AI skills without breaking the bank. With determination and these tools at your disposal, you can break into AI and uncover its potential impact on both personal and professional fronts. As you build proficiency, consider collaborating on community-driven projects to consolidate your learning and contribute to real-world solutions.

FINDING RELIABLE AI RESOURCES

Stumbling upon a myriad of online materials can feel like searching for a needle in a haystack, especially when trying to discern which resources are genuinely reliable. The tools and resources mentioned in this book have been vetted. A list of AI tools is provided after the glossary at the end of the book. As you find additional resources, ensure you are on solid ground by evaluating the authors behind the information. Check their credentials and expertise in AI. Are they recognized experts in the field? Have they published peer-reviewed articles? These inquiries help distinguish valuable insights from mere conjecture. Peer-reviewed publications are your gold standard, assuring quality and credibility.

When it comes to AI learning platforms, a few names stand out for their commitment to quality education. Coursera, edX, and Udacity offer structured courses that cater to various learning levels, providing learners with a roadmap to navigate AI's complexities. LinkedIn Learning is a robust choice for those seeking professional development, offering courses that integrate AI skills with career advancement. Each platform brings something unique to the table, ensuring you have access to comprehensive learning materials that suit your needs. Additionally, platforms like DataCamp specialize in data science and AI, offering interactive learning and practical exercises crucial for cementing AI concepts. These platforms often feature reviews and ratings, helping you gauge the course effectiveness based on past participants' experiences.

The richness of learning emerges from exploring diverse resources. Balancing theoretical knowledge with practical applications creates a well-rounded understanding of AI's potential. Engage with interactive tools and quizzes to deepen your grasp of complex topics. These hands-on experiences often cement concepts more effectively than passive reading alone. By diversifying your sources, you expose yourself to different perspectives, enhancing critical thinking and problem-solving skills. It's akin to assembling a puzzle; each piece contributes to the bigger picture. Furthermore, podcasts and videos featuring thought leaders can offer contemporary insights into emerging trends and innovations in AI.

Identifying unreliable sources takes a sharp eye and a healthy dose of skepticism. Watch out for dramatic headlines or articles that do not support their claims with evidence. Trustworthy sources usually include references or links so you can check the facts for yourself. And remember—if something sounds too perfect, it's probably not true.. Avoid materials that promise shortcuts or guaranteed mastery of AI in unrealistically short timeframes. Trust your instincts and prioritize resources that provide transparent, evidence-based information. Participating in online forums dedicated to AI can also serve as a vetting mechanism, where peers share experiences and recommendations about various learning materials and resources.

User Resource: AI Tools List

- **Coursera**: Offers comprehensive AI courses.
- **edX**: Provides access to university-level AI education.
- **Udacity**: Focuses on practical AI applications.
- **LinkedIn Learning**: Integrates AI skills with career growth.
- **Google AI**: Free courses for beginners.

These platforms and resources offer pathways into the world of AI, enabling you to build knowledge and skills confidently. By choosing wisely and investing time in credible materials, you lay a sturdy foundation for your AI journey. A complete list of AI tools with descriptions and websites is provided at the end of this book.

Chapter 3 Quiz

As you proceed in your exploration of AI, it's crucial to pause and reflect. Consider this quiz a friendly checkpoint, allowing you to evaluate your understanding and see where you stand. These questions are designed to engage your critical thinking and ensure that the concepts we have discussed resonate with you.

1. Which platform offers free courses and structured learning for AI beginners? A) YouTube, B) Coursera, C) Instagram, or D) Medium
2. What's a key advantage of using open-source AI tools? A) Expensive licensing fees, B) Limited community support, C) Accessibility without financial risk, or D) Restricted functionality.
3. Why should you diversify your AI learning sources? A) To focus solely on theoretical knowledge, B) For a balanced understanding involving practical applications, C) To avoid practical experience, or D) To rely on one source for consistency
4. How can time management tools benefit AI learners? A) By increasing the learning workload, B) By organizing schedules and maximizing efficiency, C) By requiring constant updates, or D) By providing distractions from learning
5. How does engaging with supportive learning communities aid in overcoming AI learning barriers? A) By fostering isolation in learning, B) By offering no tangible benefits, C) By providing encouragement and shared experiences, or D) By focusing on individual learning exclusively

Answers:

1-B, 2-C, 3-B, 4-B, 5-C

Your responses—especially the incorrect answers - can help identify areas you may want to revisit. Remember, this process isn't about perfection but about growth and understanding.

In Chapter 3, we tackled some of the most common barriers to learning AI, offering strategies and tools to help you navigate learning challenges with confidence. Whether it's making the most of your limited time, utilizing affordable resources, or finding reliable information, each step strengthens your foundation in AI. This chapter serves as a reminder that learning doesn't have to be daunting or expensive. With the right resources and mindset, you can embrace AI's potential in both personal and professional settings.

As we move forward into the next chapter, we'll delve into practical AI applications, bringing theory into practice in ways that enhance your daily life and work environments. Keep an open mind and remember that every step forward is progress. Let's continue exploring how AI can transform tasks and opportunities for innovation and growth.

4
AUTOMATING DAILY TASKS IN 7 DAYS

> *"Artificial intelligence, deep learning, machine learning — whatever you're doing, if you don't understand it — learn it. Because otherwise, you're going to be a dinosaur within three years."*
>
> — MARK CUBAN

DAY 1: AUTOMATE EMAIL SORTING WITH AI

We have all been there. You open your inbox to a flood of emails, each demanding your attention. It's like trying to drink from a fire hose. But what if you could transform that chaos into order with a few clicks? Enter AI-powered email management tools. These digital assistants can automatically organize and sort your emails, freeing you from the drudgery of manual sorting. Tools like SaneBox and Clean Email are game changers. They filter messages based on sender and content, prioritizing the messages of greatest importance and urgency. Imagine receiving only the emails that need your immediate attention while everything else neatly files itself away.

Setting up automation rules is simpler than you might think. Start by defining filters that align with your needs. Most email applications, like Gmail and Microsoft Outlook, allow you to assign labels to distinct categories, such as "Work," "Family," "Advertisements," or "Newsletters." This categorization helps AI understand your preferences better. Next, set up reminders for follow-ups and responses, ensuring you never miss a crucial communication. Automation rules can be tailored to include sender-specific filters, enhancing accuracy and relevance. This way, your inbox becomes a tool for productivity rather than a source of stress.

The benefits of automated email sorting are profound. Imagine the control you regain by cutting down the time spent sifting through emails, allowing you to focus on tasks that truly matter. This reduction in non-productive effort enhances efficiency, giving you more bandwidth for crucial projects and personal pursuits. By automating mundane tasks, you reclaim valuable time and mental energy. You'll immediately notice an improved ability to concentrate on high-priority communications, boosting your overall effectiveness.

As shown in the table below, several email apps offer AI tools that facilitate unsubscribing users from unwanted mailing lists.

Every new system has its hiccups, but troubleshooting can be straightforward. If filters aren't performing as expected, adjust them for better accuracy. Sometimes, simply refining keywords or adding exclusions can make a significant difference. Tweaking settings often resolves issues like false positives in spam detection, ensuring that legitimate emails aren't missed. Most AI tools offer FAQs and support resources to guide you through everyday challenges. Don't hesitate to reach out for help if needed. By addressing these minor setbacks early, you prevent frustration later and pave the way for a seamless email management experience.

Reader's Resource: Personalized Email Filter Checklist

- Define categories for emails.
- Set up sender-specific filters.
- Adjust rules for accuracy.
- Automate follow-ups and reminders.

Consider adding organizational features to customize your inbox further. Use similar strategies for sorting through newsletters or promotional emails, using AI to filter these into a separate folder where you can peruse them at leisure. Encourage users to make regular adjustments to filters and rules as needs evolve. This iterative process of refinement, common to most AI applications, ensures that your automated email sorting remains aligned with your objectives.

DAY 2: SIMPLIFYING CALENDAR MANAGEMENT AUTOMATICALLY

Imagine waking up to a perfectly orchestrated day, where every appointment and task aligns like a symphony. AI calendar tools make this possible, transforming chaotic schedules into harmonious routines. Applications like Google Calendar and Calendly offer intelligent scheduling and task reminders, ensuring you never miss a beat. With just a few keystrokes you can automate meetings and deadlines, bringing structure to your day. Setting up these recurring events is straightforward; configure them once, and they repeat effortlessly. Automated reminders keep important tasks at the forefront, nudging you when it's time to prepare or follow up.

EXAMPLE: PLACE A SCHEDULING LINK IN YOUR SIGNATURE BLOCK

Click here to schedule a meeting.

John Smith, VP – Sales
ACMECO
+1 (909) 123-4567
jsmith@acmeco-co.com

Calendly has the additional benefit of letting others schedule meetings with you in times that are open on your calendar and within windows that you designate. You can control how far in advance meetings can be scheduled, how long meetings can last, and even who receives the links to schedule meetings. A great way to use AI scheduling apps is to place a link on your personal or business website and in your email signature block as shown here, enabling interested parties to schedule a call immediately.

Calendar productivity AI tools like Trello or Asana greatly increases your efficiency. By syncing tasks and deadlines, the AI applications create seamless workflows across devices. This synchronization ensures that when you add a meeting to your calendar, related tasks update in Trello or Asana, keeping everything in sync. It's like having a personal assistant who ensures all your tools communicate flawlessly. This integrated approach streamlines your day, reducing the mental load of managing separate platforms.

A schedule organized by AI doesn't mean losing a personal touch. Customize notification settings to align with your preferences, balancing automation with your unique scheduling style. This customization prevents over-scheduling and reserves space for spontaneity and creativity. Adjust reminders to suit your rhythm, whether you prefer a gentle nudge a day or week before or a firm alert 10-15 minutes prior. These tweaks ensure that technology supports you rather than controls your life.

To avoid the pitfalls of over-automation, consider strategies that balance efficiency with flexibility. Review your automated settings to ensure they still meet your needs. Keep an eye on how much you automate—too many alerts can become noise rather than help. Periodic adjustments fine-tune your system, keeping it responsive to your evolving priorities. With AI tools, you can transform calendar chaos into calm, reclaiming time for what matters most.

DAY 3: STREAMLINING SOCIAL MEDIA WITH AI BOTS

Imagine waking up to find your social media accounts buzzing with activity, all managed effortlessly. AI bots for social media management make this a reality. They automate posting and engagement, freeing you to focus on creative activities. Tools like Buffer and Hootsuite (for large enterprises) schedule posts, ensuring content goes live when your audience is most active, and track the performance of each post. Chatbots take customer service a step further, providing instant responses to common customer questions, thus enhancing user experience without constant manual input.

Social media automation is easy to configure. Start by identifying peak engagement times for your audience; this ensures maximum reach and interaction. Configure AI bots to post during these windows. Use the bots to curate content by monitoring trends and popular topics, keeping your feed relevant and engaging. This continuous adaptation helps maintain a dynamic online presence, attracting more followers and boosting engagement rates.

Automation brings ethical considerations, particularly around authenticity. While AI can handle routine tasks, genuine interaction requires a human touch. Ensure automated responses reflect your brand's voice and values and maintain consistency across platforms. Balance automation with live engagement to avoid appearing robotic. This blend of AI efficiency and human authenticity fosters trust and loyalty among your audience.

Consider brands that have successfully integrated AI into their social media strategies. A clothing brand will use scheduled posts to showcase new collections, increasing visibility and sales. Meanwhile, a personal blogger will employ AI to curate content, gaining insight into what resonates with readers. These examples demonstrate how AI bots can amplify efforts without sacrificing quality or connection.

AI in social media management isn't just about saving time; it's about enhancing your connection with your audience. By leveraging automation tools thoughtfully, you can elevate your online presence, increase subscribership, and foster deeper relationships.

Utilize AI analytics within these tools to track the performance of your posts and refine strategies. Use insights gleaned from engagement metrics to pivot content strategies, ensuring continued audience engagement and growth.

DAY 4: AI-POWERED FINANCIAL MANAGEMENT

Wouldn't it be great to have a personal financial advisor in your pocket, ready to crunch numbers and analyze spending whenever needed? That's what AI tools for personal finance offer. Applications like Mint and You Need A Budget (YNAB) transform how you manage money, making budgeting and expense tracking almost effortless. These digital helpers categorize expenses automatically, showing where your money goes and highlighting potential savings. They analyze spending patterns, offering insights into areas ripe for trimming. With AI, managing finances becomes less about spreadsheets and more about seeing the bigger picture for your financial health.

To get started, link your bank accounts to these apps for real time updates on your spending. This integration allows for immediate tracking of transactions, providing a clear snapshot of your financial status at any moment. Alerts configured to warn when spending gets close to budget limits help maintain fiscal responsibility, providing advance notice of potential overspending. This proactive approach will help you maintain control over your finances with minimal manual input.

The benefits of automated fiscal management extend beyond convenience. AI provides insights that could otherwise go unnoticed, like recognizing subtle spending habits or identifying opportunities for savings. Automated reports offer comprehensive views of your financial health, akin to regular check-ups with a financial advisor. These features empower you to make informed decisions, fostering a deeper understanding of your financial situation.

Maximizing AI financial tools involves more than passive observation. Customize budgets within these apps to reflect personal goals and priorities. Whether saving for a vacation or paying down debt, tailor the settings to align with your objectives. Leverage AI recommendations for investment planning, using data-driven insights to guide choices in stocks or savings strategies. This personalized approach turns fiscal management into an engaging activity rather than a dreaded chore. With AI at your side, navigating the complexities of personal finance becomes an accessible and empowering experience.

To further optimize financial management, explore integrations with tax preparation software that leverage AI to simplify tax filing processes. This can streamline the preparation process and ensure compliance with relevant tax regulations.

DAY 5: USE AI TO EDIT CORRESPONDENCE AND DOCUMENTS

Imagine having a digital assistant who can polish your writing skillfully as a seasoned editor. With tools like ChatGPT and Microsoft's Copilot, this is no longer a distant dream. These general AI services offer robust capabilities for enhancing your documents. ChatGPT, for instance, can refine your drafts, suggest rephrasing, and even generate content ideas when you hit a creative block. Its adaptability makes it a versatile companion for any writing endeavor. Meanwhile, Microsoft's Copilot integrates seamlessly with Word, providing real-time suggestions that improve clarity and coherence. These tools act like your personal editorial team, helping you produce polished work effortlessly.

For more specialized editing needs, there are dedicated tools like Grammarly. It is a go-to for catching those pesky grammatical errors and ensuring your text flows smoothly. Beyond simple corrections, Grammarly also includes a plagiarism checker, offering peace of mind when you are unsure about originality. If you are venturing into publishing or academic writing, Reedsy and Scribbr can be particularly useful. Reedsy formats your book content to professional standards, readying it for publication without hassle. On the academic side, Scribbr shines by converting your citations to APA standards, streamlining the tedious task of referencing.

These AI-driven editors transform writing from a solitary task into an interactive experience. They are not just correcting; they are teaching and guiding you towards better writing practices. As you engage with these tools, you will notice an improvement in your own skills. The feedback loop they create is invaluable, fostering growth and confidence in your writing abilities. Moreover, the time saved by automating tasks can be redirected to brainstorming innovative ideas or delving deeper into research. The seamless integration of AI into the writing process allows you to focus on what truly matters—your message.

Consider utilizing AI-driven spellcheck tools for drafting in different languages or for translations, broadening your document's accessibility and reach. Engage with language-specific AI tools to refine multilingual communication skills.

DAY 6: CREATE CONTENT USING AI

Imagine sitting at your desk, needing to revamp a paragraph or generate a compelling image. That's where AI steps in, offering tools that reshape how we handle content creation. ChatGPT is exceptionally versatile. It can rewrite specific paragraphs, ensuring clarity and precision, or even install APA references by converting manuscript citations seamlessly. This tool transforms complex tasks into manageable chunks, allowing you to place greater focus on the creative aspects of developing content.

Beyond text, AI expands into visual creativity. DALL-E and Midjourney let you conjure images from mere descriptions, opening new horizons for artistic expression. Need a workbook or puzzle? AI can generate interactive content, making educational material more engaging. These capabilities are not just convenient; they redefine efficiency and creativity.

For those venturing into book publishing, specialty AI tools provide invaluable assistance. Atticus offers DIY book formatting for a onetime fee, ensuring your manuscript meets professional standards without breaking the bank. Canva, well-known for its design prowess, helps craft stunning book covers. Its Pro version unlocks even more features, enhancing your design toolkit.

Creating visuals for marketing also becomes straightforward with tools like DIY Book Covers. They produce 3D images of your book's cover across various formats, from eBooks to Kindle, boosting your promotional efforts. Similarly, Ideogram lets you generate images tailored to your specifications, giving your projects a unique flair.

Incorporating AI into content creation is not just about automation but also enhancing your ability to deliver polished, professional work. Used properly, these tools free you from mundane tasks, allowing you to channel energy into innovation and artistry. They serve as both collaborators and catalysts in your creative process. With AI's capabilities at your fingertips, the possibilities are as limitless as your imagination.

For enhanced content creation, integrate AI-driven analytics tools to evaluate content performance and user engagement. This feedback loop enables ongoing refinement and strategy adaptation, enriching the creative process.

DAY 7: PONDER THE ETHICS AND IMPLICATIONS OF AI USE

AI's integration into everyday life raises important ethical questions, especially within families. In the home, AI-powered devices like smart speakers and home assistants offer convenience but also demand vigilance in maintaining data privacy. While simplifying tasks and gathering information, these tools collect vast amounts of information, sparking debates about how much we should rely on them. For school-aged children, AI can be a learning boon, with educational apps tailoring lessons to individual needs. However, the line between helpful and invasive blurs when children's data trails become part of the equation.

In education, AI presents both opportunities and challenges. Teens and college students benefit from AI tools that assist with research and writing assignments. Yet, these tools also tempt students towards plagiarism, raising questions about academic integrity. Educators also face dilemmas as they must balance leveraging AI for personalized learning with teaching students the critical thinking skills necessary to verify information independently.

The business world sees AI as a powerful tool for streamlining operations. Administrative tasks like scheduling personnel or organizing travel arrangements become simple with AI's help. Financial functions benefit from AI's analytical prowess, identifying trends and offering insights that could go unnoticed by human analysts. However, research ethics come into play as businesses must ensure that AI does not perpetuate biases or make decisions without adequate oversight.

Governments, too, are harnessing AI for public service improvements, from traffic management to healthcare advancements. Yet, using AI in governance raises concerns about surveillance and individual freedoms. How do we balance the efficiency and benefits of AI with the need for transparency and citizen rights? Each sector faces unique ethical challenges, reminding us that while AI holds immense potential, it also requires careful consideration and responsible implementation.

Explore the ethical implications of AI's role in justice systems, highlighting potential biases in automated sentencing and the advantages of streamlining processes. Discuss AI's role in policymaking, considering how it might positively or negatively influence future governance decisions.

Chapter 4 Reader Exercises

Let's put theory into action with two practical exercises that will help you cement what you have learned about automating daily tasks using AI. These hands-on activities are designed to be simple yet effective, allowing you to experience firsthand how AI can streamline your routine.

Exercise 1: Automate a Task Using AI Tools

First, pick a task you find repetitive or time-consuming. This could be anything from scheduling social media posts to organizing files. Choose an appropriate AI tool to help automate this task. For instance, tools like Buffer or Hootsuite are great choices if you want to automate social media posts. Once you have selected your task and tool, follow these steps:

1. Set up the tool by creating an account and exploring its features.
2. Define the parameters for automation, such as timing, frequency, or specific actions.
3. Implement the automation and monitor its execution for a few days, noting any adjustments needed.

After a week, reflect on how this automation has impacted your productivity. Consider the time saved and any improvements in workflow efficiency.

Exercise 2: Analyze AI's Impact on Your Daily Routine

In this exercise, you will assess how AI influences your day-to-day tasks. Over a week, record instances where AI tools have assisted you. Examples include using AI for email management, calendar scheduling, or financial tracking. At the end of the week, analyze your findings.

1. List the AI tools you used and describe their functions.
2. Note the specific tasks they helped automate.
3. Calculate the time saved compared to manual execution.
4. Reflect on any changes in stress levels or workflow satisfaction.

These exercises reinforce your understanding of AI and illustrate its practical benefits in real-world applications. Through active engagement, you will discover AI's limitless potential for enhancing productivity and efficiency. Consider extending your analysis to include future AI usage plans based on observed benefits, creating a strategic approach to integrating AI into your daily routines moving forward.

As we wrap up Chapter 4, remember that AI is not just about technology—it's about enhancing life's quality by freeing up time for what truly matters. In Chapter 5 we explore how AI can be introduced into systems with more complexity, pushing the boundaries of what's possible in both personal and professional spheres. Prepare to delve deeper into innovative ways to embrace AI in your personal life.

5
PERSONAL PRODUCTIVITY BOOSTS WITH AI

"The real genius of AI isn't in thinking like us, but in showing us new ways to think."

— YANN LECUN, CHIEF AI SCIENTIST AT META (FORMERLY FACEBOOK)

AI FOR PERSONAL TASK MANAGEMENT

Imagine a bustling world where your overflowing to-do list quietly organizes itself, intuitively prioritizing tasks and sending reminders with the precision of a digital concierge—all without your input. This is not just a futuristic pipe dream; it's the immense power of AI-driven task management tools ready for everyday use. Platforms such as Todoist and Microsoft To Do are at the forefront of this revolution, reshaping how we tackle daily responsibilities. By scrutinizing your historical behavior, these apps intelligently prioritize tasks, ensuring you concentrate on what truly requires your attention. They adapt and learn from your routines, suggesting optimal times for task completion, making your schedule feel less of a burden and more of an orchestrated symphony.

Initiating automated reminders and alerts is a straightforward endeavor. Begin by setting up personalized alerts for upcoming tasks. Whether managing a deadline for your latest project or scheduling time to gather weekly groceries, AI secures that no detail escapes unnoticed. Start by syncing your calendar with these proficient task management apps; this integration offers a seamless experience, leading to a cohesive overview of your commitments. Customize alert settings to match your style—like a gentle nudge a day ahead or a decisive alert 15 minutes prior. This tailored approach empowers you to stay on top of your tasks without feeling overwhelmed by too many notifications.

The advantages of AI in task management transcend mere convenience. These tools ease the mental load required for organizing tasks by automating prioritization based on urgency and importance. Envision waking to daily or weekly summaries of your task progress, neatly compiled by AI. This feature conserves time and grants clarity about upcoming responsibilities, making planning more accessible. Automation of mundane organizational chores liberates cognitive space, permitting you to focus on tasks demanding creativity and critical thinking.

As with traditional project management tools, optimizing task management with AI demands a committed approach. Diligently update your task lists and promptly mark completed items. Maintaining this habit ensures the AI algorithms have the freshest data to improve their predictions and recommendations. Harness AI analytics to gain insights into your productivity trends. These tools can reveal peak productivity periods, assisting you in allocating your time more judiciously. Apply these insights to adjust your workflow, maximizing efficiency without the anxiety of micromanagement.

Reader's Resource: Task Management Optimization Checklist

- Regularly update task lists and completion statuses.
- Set up custom reminders and alerts for deadlines.
- Integrate calendar events with task management tools.
- Use AI analytics to identify peak productivity hours.
- Adjust workflows based on AI-generated insights.
- Review and refine task management strategies monthly.

ENHANCING PERSONAL CREATIVITY WITH AI TOOLS

In the vibrant sphere of creativity, AI tools function like having an additional pair of creative hands—or perhaps a muse softly guiding your inspiration. Picture yourself as a visual artist, standing before a blank canvas, unsure of your initial brush-stroke. With the support of tools such as DALL-E, you can conjure breathtaking visual art from uncomplicated text prompts, igniting your inspiration and providing a launchpad for your creative journey. These applications transcend the limits of visual arts; AI music composition software enables you to compose unique pieces, transforming raw ideas into melodies and harmonies that resonate with your distinct style.

Incorporating AI into your creative workflow does not mean compromising your artistic vision. It is about augmenting it. Consider employing AI for brainstorming when you encounter inevitable creative blocks. These tools can propose new perspectives, offering innovative angles that restart your imagination. The injection of AI-generated elements into your projects introduces an extra layer of innovation, pushing the boundaries and uncovering concepts you might not have previously contemplated. Whether designing a new layout or penning a novel, these AI inputs can act as a catalyst for further creativity.

The impact of AI on creative output is absolutely trailblazing. Picture engaging in a graphic design endeavor with access to AI-generated templates providing a professional-grade foundation. This process saves valuable time and elevates your work's overall quality. For authors, collaborating with AI can lead to expanded narratives and more engaging dialogues. Envision being stuck on a plot twist; an AI suggestion could provide the missing piece that cohesively ties everything together.

Real-life narratives illustrate how individuals harness AI to expand their creative boundaries further than ever before. A freelance designer might use AI to generate innovative art pieces, harmonizing algorithmic suggestions with a personal touch to craft something genuinely original. Meanwhile, a writer can delve into plot development with AI recommendations, breathing new life into stories that previously languished. These instances demonstrate that AI does not overshadow human creativity but complements it—acting as both a tool and a collaborator in the creative journey.

The realm of creativity is evolving as AI becomes more seamlessly integrated into artistic processes. It opens doors previously constrained by time or skill limitations, allowing you to concentrate on the essence of creation rather than the mechanics. As you explore these tools, remember that AI's role is to support and amplify your vision rather than overshadow it. Embrace the vast opportunities it offers to enrich your creative endeavors, redefining the boundaries of possibility in art, design, and storytelling.

USING AI FOR EFFICIENT TIME MANAGEMENT

Envision having an assistant who manages your schedule and evolves with your habits to optimize your day. AI-driven scheduling assistants like x.ai and Clockwise serve this purpose, intelligently arranging meetings and allocating time, ensuring your day progresses smoothly. These tools analyze your past activities, suggest the prime times for task completion, and help eliminate those pesky scheduling conflicts that hamper productivity.

AI time management strategies are easy to establish. Begin by designating periods for focused work and essential breaks. This structured method helps prevent burnout and fosters concentration. Employ AI to automate meeting schedules based on your availability, sparing you the tediousness of incessant back-and-forth emails. Simply input your preferences, and let the system handle the rest. This saves time and reduces the stress associated with manual scheduling.

The many benefits of AI in time management are both compelling and effective. By automating scheduling, you mitigate conflicts and overlaps, optimizing your calendar's efficiency. Intelligent time allocation ensures a better work-life balance, preventing overcommitment. With AI's skillful assistance, you are able to reserve specific hours for work tasks without encroaching on personal time, achieving a harmonious blend of productivity and relaxation.

To optimize AI's benefits in time management, consider adopting strategic habits. Consistently review AI-generated time reports to comprehend how you spend your day. These insights reveal patterns and highlight areas where you can enhance efficiency. Assign time limits for tasks to prevent them from expanding unnecessarily, encourage focus and dedication, and ensure task completion within designated periods.

AI-powered tools provide a unique perspective on our time usage. They present a framework that simplifies decision-making and enhances productivity by automating routine tasks. Equipped with these tools, managing time transcends juggling responsibilities; it becomes about optimizing opportunities. Whether you are a busy professional or a multitasking student, AI can revolutionize your daily approach, enabling you to achieve more with less exertion.

AI tools also identify time-wasting activities that slyly infiltrate our routines. Automated time-tracking tools expose where your minutes slip away, allowing you to reclaim them for higher priority and more fulfilling pursuits. By understanding your time allocation, informed decisions about prioritizing activities and minimizing distractions become straightforward.

Intelligent scheduling assistants do not merely organize; they anticipate needs and adapt to real-time changes. If meetings run over or plans shift, these tools autonomously adjust your schedule, maintaining equilibrium without external intervention. This flexibility ensures your schedule remains resilient and neatly ordered - even during chaotic episodes.

Incorporating AI into daily routines involves keeping an open mind and a willingness to embrace technology's promises. These tools are designed to work with you, offering support that adjusts to your unique requirements. By capitalizing on AI's capabilities, you streamline your day, enhance productivity, and relish a sense of control over your schedule that once seemed elusive.

As you explore these AI solutions, keep in mind that they are more than just tools—they are partners in your journey toward greater efficiency. Bringing them into your daily routines allows you to take control of your time, turning it from a constraint into a powerful asset that drives success.

AI SOLUTIONS FOR PERSONAL ORGANIZATION

Picture a clutter-free digital existence where every document is right at your fingertips, effortlessly organized, and instantly accessible. AI tools have revolutionized how we manage personal information, transforming chaos into order. Consider Evernote and Notion—two robust applications that streamline digital note taking and organization. They assist in categorizing and tagging notes, making retrieval a seamless process. With AI-powered document management systems, organizing files becomes second nature. These systems astutely sort documents, ensuring everything is filed correctly and nothing gets lost amid the shuffle.

Implementing AI personal organization strategies is akin to employing a digital personal assistant. Start by automating document categorization and tagging. Set up rules dictating where files should go based on their content; for example, invoices automatically file under "Finance," while meeting notes fall under "Work." This automation saves time and minimizes human error, allowing you to concentrate on more significant endeavors. The creation of AI-driven reminders for task deadlines and calendar events is equally straightforward. Link your calendar to these AI tools so crucial dates never fade from memory. Customized alerts keep you informed, guaranteeing you are prepared for future commitments.

The many advantages of AI in personal organization are numerous and substantial. Advanced search capabilities mean you can locate documents or notes with a simple keyword search, significantly reducing time spent sifting through files. Imagine seeking a specific piece of information—you type a few words, and there it is. Automated archiving and backup solutions secure your data, offering peace of mind against technical failures. These features guard your work and ensure it is readily accessible whenever necessary.

Stories of individuals revolutionizing their organizational habits with AI are inspiring. Take Sarah, a freelance writer who was overwhelmed by managing her research notes and deadlines. By adopting Notion, she transformed her workflow—organizing notes by project, syncing deadlines with her calendar, and setting reminders before each milestone. Then there's Mark, an entrepreneur who employed an AI-powered document management system to handle his business files. The automated sorting and tagging unburdened him from manual filing, allowing him more time to focus on strategic decisions.

AI solutions for personal organization are about more than tidying up digital spaces; they are about enhancing your ability to manage information. Whether you are a student juggling multiple assignments or a professional handling various projects, these tools offer a streamlined approach to organization and task management. They minimize clutter and maximize efficiency by enabling quick and reliable information retrieval. With AI by your side, personal organization becomes less of a hassle and more of an empowering experience.

The integration of AI strategies into your daily routine doesn't demand replacing your existing tools and systems—it's about making gradual improvements that lead to substantial results. By leveraging AI's capabilities, you can customize an organizational system to evolve with your needs. As technology progresses, these tools will become indispensable when navigating modern information management complexities.

Chapter 5 Reader Exercise

The following exercises will help you implement AI tools in your daily life, enhancing productivity and creativity. Let's explore two exercises designed for practical AI application.

Begin by choosing a task you frequently undertake, such as organizing digital photos or managing a weekly grocery list. Use an AI tool like Google Photos or AnyList to automate this task. Google Photos employs AI to categorize images by location, date, and subject, simplifying the future search for specific photos. For grocery lists, AnyList offers intelligent suggestions based on past shopping patterns, ensuring no items are forgotten. Dedicate thirty minutes to exploring these features and tweaking settings to best suit your requirements.

Next, track your daily time allocation, identifying where AI might save valuable minutes. Use a digital notepad or spreadsheet to record activities and durations. Identify tasks that are repetitive or time-consuming. Once identified, research AI tools that are designed to optimize these tasks. For example, if emails consume copious amounts of time, explore AI email assistants that adeptly sort and prioritize your inbox. Spend a week observing the impact of these tools on your workflow, noting any productivity enhancements. This reflection will highlight where AI delivers the most significant value.

As we conclude Chapter 5, take a moment to reflect on how AI enhances both productivity and creativity. From task management to schedule optimization, AI presents tools that streamline daily activities, freeing time for what truly matters. These exercises aim to demonstrate how practical AI applications can alleviate life's daily demands, simplifying complex processes. Our next chapter will explore more advanced topics, delving into how businesses and industries harness AI for strategic growth and innovation.

CAN I COUNT ON YOU?

"We make a living by what we get, but we make a life by what we give."

— *WINSTON CHURCHILL*

Hi there!

If you've made it to this page, I want to say **thank you**. You've spent time learning, exploring, and maybe even starting to use AI to make your life easier. That's a big deal!

When I first started using AI, I had no idea what to do. I was just trying to stop wasting so much time. Now, here I am—sharing what I've learned so that **you** can save time too.

If this book helped you—even just a little—I'd love it if you could **leave a quick review**.

Here's why it matters:

- **Your review helps others.** Just as you once wondered, "Is this book really for me?", someone else is wondering the same thing. Your words can help them decide to give it a try.
- **It helps me keep going.** Every review tells me that this work matters and gives me energy to write more guides like this for beginners like you.
- **You are paying it forward.** A review is free to give, but its impact can be huge.

You don't need to write anything fancy. A few honest words—what you liked, what worked for you, or how AI helped you this week—go a long way. Better yet, **use AI to write a review!** I will even provide some prompts:

... I finally understand what all the AI hype is about

...didn't know AI could be so easy to use

...now I want to learn more to stay ahead of my peers

To share your thoughts, simply scan the QR code below or navigate to:

https://amazon.com/review-your-purchases/?asin=

Thanks again for reading. I hope this is just the beginning of what you'll do with AI.

—Wesley Thomas

👋 *P.S. It only takes a minute, and it really does make a difference.*

6

AI IN PROFESSIONAL SETTINGS

"It's replacing us in the workforce—not in the future, but now."

— JON STEWART, ON *THE DAILY SHOW*

AUTOMATING PROJECT MANAGEMENT TASKS

Picture the chaos of juggling multiple projects, each with distinct timelines, resource requirements, and varying stakeholder inputs. Now, imagine a sophisticated tool that orchestrates these components, allowing you to focus on strategic goals rather than getting bogged down in the minutiae of daily tasks. AI is at the forefront of revolutionizing project management, transforming this vision into a practical reality. Platforms like Monday.com and ClickUp lead the charge, offering innovative automated task assignments that adapt in real time to team members' skills and availability. These tools use AI algorithms to analyze workload distributions, efficiently assigning tasks and consistently completing them on schedule.

Furthermore, these AI platforms are equipped with machine learning capabilities that can refine task distribution patterns based on past performance data, enabling a more intuitive allocation of responsibilities over time. For instance, by reviewing historical project data, the system can recognize which team members excel at particular types of tasks and automatically adjust future assignments to maximize efficiency. This proactive approach enhances productivity and fosters a collaborative environment where team strengths are systematically leveraged.

AI-driven project timelines can be established without great difficulty, even for those without extensive technical skills. Begin by inputting your project details into the platform of choice. Monday.com, for instance, involves entering deadlines, specifying dependencies, and acknowledging available resources. The AI then takes the reins, generating smart Gantt charts that outline your project's progress trajectory. These charts are dynamic, updating in real-time as team members log their progress or as resource availability shifts, essentially serving as a living document that evolves alongside your project. This capability for dynamic adjustment means you are never caught off guard by sudden alterations or resource bottlenecks.

Consider implementing a feedback loop where team members can provide insights into AI tool performance. Such a mechanism will help fine-tune project algorithms, ensuring the automated processes align closely with team dynamics and evolving project needs. Through continuous refinement, AI in project management can adapt to both the subtle complexities of human behavior and the shifting landscapes of business objectives.

The benefits of automating tasks in project management are tangible and wide-ranging. Firstly, it significantly reduces manual workloads. Rather than spending countless hours on repetitive scheduling, you can direct your attention to high-impact, strategic initiatives. AI also tracks progress automatically and sends timely reminders about upcoming deadlines, ensuring nothing slips through the gaps. Moreover, AI provides critical insights into resource allocation, suggesting proactive adjustments to mitigate risks and optimize efficiency. Envision having a virtual project manager that not only tracks but also predicts potential hurdles, empowering you to navigate around them before they become serious issues.

Consider the success stories of teams effectively utilizing AI for project management. Take the tech startup, for instance, which used AI tools to streamline its sprint planning process. By aligning tasks with team capacities, the platform facilitated more efficient execution and swifter iterations. Similarly, a marketing team leveraged AI to automate campaign timelines, resulting in a more agile approach that enabled them to pivot strategies based on real-time data, without missing a beat. These examples underscore how AI can transform project management from a tedious chore into an innovative, intelligent process.

Interactive Element: Project Automation Checklist

- Identify key tasks suitable for automation.
- Input project details into an AI tool like Monday.com.
- Set up automated schedules with real-time updates.
- Regularly review AI-generated insights for adjustments.

ENHANCING WORKPLACE COMMUNICATION WITH AI

Visualize a workplace where communication flows seamlessly, effortlessly transcending language barriers and meeting intricacies. AI transforms this vision into reality by facilitating clear and efficient communication across professional settings. Tools like Otter.ai have redefined how we capture meeting notes. Instead of frenetic scribbling, it transcribes conversations in real time, allowing participants to remain engaged and focused. Real-time translation tools further elevate international collaboration by dissolving language barriers, ensuring messages are comprehended accurately, and facilitating smoother interactions across diverse teams.

Moreover, AI-driven platforms like Grammarly have become essential tools for crafting clear, concise, and grammatically sound communications. Such tools rectify linguistic errors and offer style enhancements, accommodating diverse writing styles. Power BI has transformed data visualization into an art form, turning raw numbers into vivid, comprehendible visualizations that tell compelling stories. AI-driven predictive analytics take things a step further, forecasting trends and equipping you with the foresight needed to anticipate changes before they unfold. This goes beyond mere number crunching; it's about transforming data into a narrative that guides strategic decision-making.

Further enriching this environment, AI-integrated anomaly detection capabilities add substantial value. These enhancements aid in identifying irregularities in data patterns that may signify potential disruptions or untapped opportunities. For a financial analyst, such a tool could flag unexpected market aberrations, allowing for preemptive measures in investment strategies. This proactive stance ensures that you stay reactive and possess the vision to stay ahead of the competitive curve.

At first, establishing AI data workflows might feel like piecing together a complex puzzle, but the bigger picture emerges with clarity once the components align. Start by connecting your data sources to an AI platform, ensuring real-time updates flow seamlessly. This integration lets you monitor critical performance indicators on dynamic dashboards, tailored to adapt to your business needs. With a few clicks, you can automate data collection and analysis, freeing you from the tedium of manual data entry and safeguarding accuracy throughout the process. These dashboards act as your command center, providing a panoramic view of your operations.

The advantages of AI in data analysis extend beyond mere efficiency. AI delves into datasets to unearth insights, identifying patterns and anomalies that may go unnoticed. Imagine detecting a subtle trend indicating a shift in consumer behavior or spotting an anomaly representing a potential risk. AI facilitates the automatic generation of reports, crafting comprehensive presentations for stakeholders and allowing you to concentrate on strategy rather than spreadsheets. This capability boosts productivity and empowers you with the confidence to make informed, data-driven decisions.

Consider the narrative of a retail company that adopted AI for inventory management. By analyzing sales patterns and seasonal variations, they optimized stock levels and minimized waste, resulting in significant cost savings. Similarly, a financial institution utilized AI for risk assessment, proactively identifying vulnerabilities and mitigating potential threats before they escalated. These examples illustrate how businesses can capitalize on AI to turn challenges into opportunities, driving innovation and success in their fields.

Further enhancing the strategic deployment of AI in data analysis, consider integrating machine learning models that learn from historical data points to improve forecasting accuracy, whether in predicting market trends or enhancing customer satisfaction metrics. This ongoing learning process ensures your data strategies are not static but evolve to provide increasingly accurate predictive insights.

SUCCESSFUL DATA ANALYSIS CASE STUDIES

• Walmart: Optimizing Inventory Management with AI

Walmart leverages AI-powered data analysis to manage its massive global inventory. By analyzing historical sales data, seasonal trends, and local buying behavior, the company's AI systems accurately forecast demand at the store level. This enables real-time inventory adjustments, reduces overstock and stock outs, and enhances overall supply chain efficiency.

• JP Morgan Chase: AI for Enhanced Risk Assessment

JP Morgan Chase implemented AI-driven risk analytics to monitor and flag irregular financial transactions. By using natural language processing (NLP) and machine learning algorithms, their system scans millions of documents and transaction records to identify fraud risks and compliance issues faster than traditional methods—protecting billions in assets and avoiding regulatory penalties.

Transforming Strategy Through AI-Driven Analysis

The inclusion of AI in your data analysis strategy does more than streamline workflows—it revolutionizes decision-making. AI tools can uncover patterns invisible to human analysts, predict future trends with greater precision, and automate insights that once required days of manual work.

Whether you are managing logistics for a retail empire or mitigating financial risk, AI gives you a strategic advantage. By embracing these technologies, you don't just keep up with innovation—you lead it. Use of these tools and techniques allows you to keep pace with technological advancements and to position yourself at the forefront of innovation.

AI-DRIVEN DECISION MAKING

Imagine facing a critical business decision, surrounded by a mountain of data. The sheer volume can be overwhelming, but AI transforms this chaos into clarity, providing the insights necessary to make informed choices. In professional settings, AI serves as a vital support for decision-making processes, analyzing data to reveal patterns and predict potential outcomes. Algorithms specifically designed for scenario planning enable you to explore various possibilities and their potential impacts, helping you anticipate both challenges and opportunities. Tools focusing on risk analysis and strategic planning offer a clear roadmap, guiding you through complex decisions with increased confidence.

As you harness AI's decision-making potential, consider incorporating machine perceptiveness, which involves AI systems refining their analyses based on user feedback. Your interactive engagement adds a human layer to AI's logic, fine-tuning its outcomes to align more closely with your strategic objectives. This collaboration between human intuition and AI precision ensures that your decision-making framework continuously adapts and remains relevant in fluctuating business environments.

Incorporating AI insights into decision frameworks involves setting up real-time dashboards that provide critical information at a glance. These dashboards spotlight key performance indicators, empowering you to make swift, informed adjustments, as necessary. Configuring alerts for pivotal decision points ensures that you remain vigilant and responsive; when specific thresholds are met, the system notifies you, prompting timely action. Imagine a consultant who works tirelessly around the clock, providing data-driven recommendations and relieving you from the guesswork. This integration simplifies processes, making decisions faster and more accurate.

The benefits of AI-enhanced decision-making are also evident in their ability to reduce uncertainty. With AI's predictive capabilities, you can adapt to market changes with agility, maintaining a competitive edge. Enhanced precision in forecasts and projections minimizes risks, allowing for more effective resource allocation. Envision knowing the likely outcomes of a business strategy before its implementation—AI provides that foresight. It's like possessing a crystal ball that translates vague possibilities into actionable plans, strengthening confidence in your decisions.

Consider organizations that have successfully harnessed AI to steer strategic decisions. Logistics companies use AI to optimize delivery routes, considering traffic patterns and weather conditions, thereby enhancing scheduling efficiency and end customer satisfaction. Manufacturers employ AI for quality control and for predicting equipment failures before they occur, reducing downtime and costs. These examples demonstrate the ability of AI to convert complex data into actionable insights that propel success.

In optimizing your approach to using AI, consider utilizing AI simulations to test various business scenarios. This provides a risk-free environment where potential strategies can be tested and evaluated before full-scale implementation. This experimental space allows creative exploration and innovation while safeguarding your organization from potential pitfalls.

To explore further, contemplate how AI might revolutionize your decision-making processes. Whether it involves predicting consumer behavior or optimizing supply chains, the potential applications are vast and varied. By embracing AI, you open the door to a realm where data shifts from a formidable challenge to a strategic asset. With the right tools and strategies, you can traverse the complexities of modern business with clarity and confidence, allowing technology to enhance your decision-making capabilities.

Chapter 6 Reader Exercise

Let us delve into two practical exercises that will make AI more tangible and beneficial in professional settings. These activities focus on integrating AI into everyday work tasks, thus enhancing productivity and decision-making skills.

Exercise #1: Explore using AI to automate administrative tasks. Consider those repetitive, time-consuming duties such as scheduling meetings, managing email inflow, or organizing digital files. AI solutions can take the helm here, liberating your time for more strategic endeavors. Select an AI assistant such as x.ai to automate meeting arrangements. Initiate the setup by integrating your calendar and specifying preferences related to availability and meeting types. Experiment with different configurations to witness how seamlessly it integrates with your workflow. Observe how the tool manages scheduling conflicts and proposes alternative times.

This adaptability is paradigm-shifting in bustling environments.

Exercise #2: Ponder AI's potential to enhance your data analysis capabilities. If you spend hours sifting through reports or compiling data insights, AI will radically improve this process. Tools like Microsoft Power BI offer a streamlined approach by auto-generating visual reports based on real-time data. Begin by linking your data sources—sales figures, customer feedback, or performance metrics—to the AI platform. Then, experiment with creating customized dashboards to highlight key metrics. This setup enables the effortless monitoring of trends and anomalies. Notice how AI identifies patterns and presents them with clarity, offering insights that would otherwise remain buried within intricate datasets.

To fully grasp the potential of these AI tools, try blending both exercises in a project scenario. Imagine leading a team tasked with launching a new product. Utilize x.ai to coordinate team meetings efficiently, ensuring everyone stays synchronized without the typical back-and-forth associated with scheduling. Concurrently, employ Power BI to analyze market data and customer feedback, tailoring your strategic approach based on AI-driven insights. This interaction between automation and data analysis vividly demonstrates how AI can elevate your professional competencies.

As you engage with these exercises, document the advantages you encounter. Reflect on AI's impact on efficiency and your decision-making process. Do tasks now feel more manageable? Has it brought to light insights previously unconsidered? Utilize these reflections to fine-tune your approach, ensuring optimal value extraction from AI's capabilities.

Engage further with AI-driven content creation tools such as Jasper for drafting reports or presentations. AI can assist in compiling and organizing content tailored to your audience, enhancing the coherence and impact of your communications.

In concluding Chapter 6, we've unpacked how AI can redefine professional landscapes by automating mundane tasks, enhancing communication, and transforming decision-making. Each element contributes to a more efficient, insightful workplace where technology supports rather than eclipses human potential. As we transition to the forthcoming chapter, we will explore the ethical implications of AI use, examining how to balance technological progress with responsibility and integrity. These insights will provide a comprehensive understanding of AI's role in modern workplaces, ensuring you have the knowledge and acumen to apply it effectively.

7
CREATIVE APPLICATIONS OF AI

"Machines excel at computation, but humans excel at creativity. That's where we must focus."

— DEMIS HASSABIS, AI PIONEER AND CO-FOUNDER OF DEEPMIND

DESIGNING WITH AI: FROM CANVA TO MIDJOURNEY

Imagine sitting in your art studio, staring at a blank canvas, eager to create something stunning but unsure where to begin. This is where AI-driven design tools like Canva and Midjourney can be useful, easily and efficiently transforming design dreams into reality. Canva's intuitive drag-and-drop interface allows even the novice designer to craft professional graphics effortlessly. It's akin to wielding an entire design team right at your fingertips, offering a myriad of templates for everything from social media posts to marketing materials. On the other hand, Midjourney elevates creativity by generating unique visual art. Its AI capabilities allow for creating intricate designs that would take hours manually, amplifying artistic potential in unprecedented ways.

Our journey through these tools begins with exploring Canva's extensive library of templates. You can select from numerous pre-designed layouts tailored for platforms like Instagram, Facebook, and LinkedIn. Once you have chosen a template as a starting point, customization is in your hands. Adjust colors, fonts, and images to align with your vision. Canva's AI assists by suggesting elements that enhance your design cohesively, considering current design trends and best practices for visual hierarchy, and providing insights that help create pleasing compositions. Midjourney takes a different approach by letting you input concepts or styles you wish to explore. It then generates art that pushes creative boundaries, offering fresh perspectives you might not have considered and leading to surprising and delightful results.

The democratization of design through AI tools is revolutionary. You no longer need years of experience or expensive software to produce high-quality content. These tools provide a quick turnaround for projects, making completing tasks in hours rather than days feasible. They grant access to advanced features traditionally reserved for professionals, unlocking creativity for anyone willing to explore their artistic side. Whether branding a small business or crafting artwork for personal projects, AI supports your journey by streamlining the process, providing inspiration and technical support simultaneously, and facilitating a seamless transition from concept to creation.

Consider the thousands of small business owners who utilized Canva's logo maker to establish a brand identity. With minimal cost and time, they crafted a logo that resonated with their target audience, enhancing their market presence. Meanwhile, artists have embraced Midjourney to expand their portfolios, using AI-generated art to explore new styles and concepts, often combining them with traditional methods for striking outcomes. These examples highlight how AI is not just a tool but a partner in the creative process, enabling impactful designs without the usual constraints. Moreover, educational institutions have started incorporating these tools into their curricula, teaching students the power of technology in artistic expression, which prepares them for a future where digital fluency will be as important as traditional skills. Such integration exemplifies the shift toward embracing technology as a fundamental aspect of modern education, broadening students' horizons and equipping them with practical skills for future endeavors.

Resources for Readers: Design Inspiration Checklist

- Explore existing templates for initial ideas.
- Customize elements like colors and fonts to reflect your brand's uniqueness.
- Use AI-generated suggestions for enhancement and insight into emerging trends.
- Experiment with assorted styles in Midjourney for unique art expressions.
- Integrate traditional design principles with AI innovations for a balanced approach.

These tools revolutionize how we approach design, making creativity accessible and achievable for everyone. The landscape of digital creativity is evolving, with AI acting as a catalyst that encourages innovation and daring, novel approaches. AI inspires users to break free from conventional design limitations and explore innovative dimensions of visual artistry.

WRITING ASSISTANCE WITH TOOLS LIKE GRAMMARLY

Picture this: You are staring at your screen with an idea but struggling to find the right words to express your thoughts clearly. This is where AI-powered writing tools like Grammarly emerge, elevating your writing quality and efficiency. Grammarly offers real-time suggestions that refine grammar and enhance style, ensuring your message hits the mark. Beyond catching typos, it provides stylistic suggestions to improve tone and clarity, adapting to your unique writing voice. Its AI-driven plagiarism detector checks for originality, adding a crucial layer of integrity for both academic and professional writing. With Grammarly, you gain a digital writing assistant that transforms rough drafts into polished prose, freeing up mental space to focus on the core message you want to convey, enhancing communication effectiveness across various contexts.

It is easy and highly rewarding to add Grammarly into your writing process. Start by setting up Grammarly's extension or desktop app for seamless integration across platforms like email and word processors. Tailor the tool to your needs by configuring style preferences—choose formal or casual tones depending on the context. Its tone detectors ensure your message resonates with the intended audience, whether you are crafting a business proposal or a personal blog post. By providing personalized feedback, Grammarly helps you recognize patterns in your writing habits, turning mistakes into learning opportunities. This setup turns everyday writing tasks into skill-building exercises, fostering a greater appreciation for linguistic precision and elegance, and ultimately nurturing language mastery.

The advantages of using AI in writing are manifold. Consistency becomes second nature as Grammarly ensures a unified voice across all documents, whether you are drafting emails or compiling reports. It enhances clarity, making complex ideas accessible to diverse audiences without sacrificing depth. This tool doesn't just polish; it teaches. As you receive feedback, you inadvertently develop a keener eye for detail and a stronger command of language nuances. Grammarly acts as both critic and coach, elevating your current work and overall writing acumen, helping individuals evolve into more proficient and confident communicators.

Consider the case of a student struggling to compose an essay. By leveraging Grammarly's suggestions, her essays transformed from incoherent collections of thoughts into structured and compelling arguments. In another case, a professional writing persuasive business proposals found that AI insights helped sharpen her pitches, resulting in more successful outcomes. These examples illustrate how AI-enhanced writing tools empower individuals to achieve better results without extensive training or costly resources. The real magic lies in how these tools bridge the gap between intent and expression, offering support exactly where it is needed. In addition to academic and business contexts, creative writers have discovered that Grammarly assists in maintaining narrative flow and thematic coherence, which are crucial for engaging storytelling.

Reader's Resource: Writing Improvement Checklist

- Install Grammarly for your browser and desktop for comprehensive coverage.
- Set up personal style preferences to ensure alignment with your writing goals.

- Use tone detectors for varied contexts to engage different audiences effectively.
- Review feedback for continuous improvement and deeper insight into writing dynamics.
- Incorporate AI suggestions into daily writing routines to enhance linguistic skills.

With AI writing help, putting thoughts into words becomes less daunting and more rewarding. As Grammarly evolves, it adapts to the changing landscape of digital communication, ensuring that users remain at the forefront of articulate expression. This adaptability ensures that writers of all calibers can enjoy a seamless writing experience, facilitating better communication in both personal and professional spheres.

AI-POWERED ART WITH DALL-E

Imagine a world where your most unorthodox artistic ideas can take shape with just a few typed words. That's the magic of DALL-E, a groundbreaking AI tool that generates art from textual descriptions. Whether crafting surreal landscapes or abstract concepts, DALL-E opens the door to limitless creative possibilities. This tool doesn't just replicate; it innovates, producing imaginative and unique images. It's like having an artist at your command, ready to bring your visions to life with precision and flair. The potential applications for DALL-E extend beyond traditional art, influencing industries such as marketing, product design, and even urban planning by providing visualizations that align closely with conceptual designs, thus revolutionizing how visual concepts are brought to life.

Getting started with DALL-E is an adventure in creativity. Begin by crafting detailed prompts that guide the AI in generating art that is aligned with your vision. Want a painting of a futuristic cityscape at dawn? Describe it vividly, specifying elements like color palettes or stylistic influences. As DALL-E generates images, iterate on these creations, tweaking descriptions to refine and develop new concepts. This process isn't just about output; it's a collaboration between human intuition and machine ingenuity, sparking ideas you might never have considered alone. This dynamic process enhances your ability to envision and articulate creative goals, fostering an exploratory mindset that emboldens you to take creative risks and discover innovative solutions to artistic challenges.

AI's impact on art is profound, breaking down barriers and expanding creative boundaries. Traditional techniques blend seamlessly with AI innovations, encouraging artists to experiment and explore unique artistic directions. This fusion of old and new fosters diversity in expression, allowing for unique combinations that challenge conventional norms. AI doesn't replace the artist's touch; it enhances it, providing tools that push the limits of imagination and technique, thus redefining the boundaries of what art can achieve.

Consider the story of an artist Suhail Doshi who curated a gallery exhibition in San Francisco featuring AI-generated pieces crafted with DALL-E. The exhibition captivated audiences, showcasing a blend of human creativity and AI innovation that provoked thought and discussion. In another example, designers in gaming and film industries use DALL-E for concept art, generating visual motifs that set the tone for entire projects. These stories highlight how AI-driven art isn't just a novelty; it's a pivotal force shaping modern creative landscapes. Furthermore, educators are now employing DALL-

E as a teaching aid in art schools, demonstrating the capabilities of AI to inspire new generations of artists by offering exposure to various artistic interpretations and styles. This exposure fosters an appreciation for digital artistry, encouraging students to experiment and innovate beyond traditional artistic boundaries.

Reader's Resource: Guide to Crafting Prompts for Creativity Tools

- Specify detailed descriptions for better accuracy in capturing your artistic vision.
- Incorporate stylistic references for tailored outcomes that align with desired aesthetics.
- Iterate on initial outputs to refine ideas and achieve a polished final product.
- Experiment with various themes to fuel creativity and explore different narrative paths.
- Leverage AI-generated insights to challenge creative norms and innovate new expressions.

The tool's potential is vast, inspiring artists to rethink what's possible in art creation. The interaction between human creativity and machine learning fosters a unique artistic environment where innovation thrives. Artists are encouraged to explore uncharted territories in digital art, blending traditional and modern techniques to pioneer novel forms of creative expression that captivate audiences worldwide.

AI IN MUSIC AND VIDEO CREATION

Imagine sitting at your computer, the cursor blinking, waiting for inspiration. But instead of staring at a blank screen, you have AI tools like Amper Music ready to transform your musical ideas into reality. Amper Music allows you to generate custom soundtracks tailored to your specific needs, whether it's a dramatic score for a video or a background tune for a podcast. You choose the mood and genre, and the AI composes music that aligns with your vision. It's like having a personal composer who never tires and is always ready to create something new. Regardless of one's musical training, this capability empowers anyone to produce professional-grade music that enhances their projects, extending creative possibilities to those without traditional musical backgrounds.

Similarly, AI is revolutionizing video editing by simplifying the entire process. Tools like Magisto use AI algorithms to analyze raw footage, automatically selecting the best clips and arranging them into cohesive narratives. You no longer need to be a seasoned editor to produce compelling videos. This software even adds transitions and effects that elevate the quality of your content effortlessly. It's as if you have hired a professional editor who works tirelessly to bring your vision to life. The integration of AI in video production means you can focus on storytelling while the technical aspects of editing are handled seamlessly behind the scenes. This efficiency reduces the time spent on tweaking projects and allows you to dedicate more energy to creativity, fostering a more fluid and engaging creative process.

The benefits of incorporating AI into music and video creation are clear. By cutting down the time and effort required for editing and composing, creators can focus on refining their craft rather than getting bogged down by technical details. These tools provide access to features that were once exclusive to industry professionals, democratizing the creation process and allowing anyone with an idea to produce high-quality multimedia content. This means that barriers to entry are lowered, opening up opportunities for more voices and talents to be heard and seen in the creative landscape, enabling a more inclusive and diverse range of creative expressions.

Consider the story of an indie filmmaker who used AI-driven tools to score and edit their short film. With limited resources, he managed to create a piece that resonated well with audiences, earning accolades at film festivals. The ability of AI to streamline and enhance multimedia projects has proven invaluable in allowing creators to focus on their narrative and artistic expression rather than getting lost in the complexities of production. Beyond indie filmmakers, businesses leverage AI in their marketing campaigns, creating engaging video ads and branded content that captivate audiences and deliver impactful messages. This enhances brand visibility and connects with audiences on a more personal level, fostering deeper engagement and loyalty.

Chapter 7 Reader Quiz

AI is reshaping how we interact with creativity, offering tools that enhance and transform the artistic process. But how well do you grasp the concepts we've covered? This quiz will help you reflect on your knowledge, ensuring you have absorbed the essentials from our exploration of AI's creative applications. Ready to test your understanding? Let's see how much you have picked up.

1. True or False: AI tools like Grammarly only correct basic spelling errors.
2. True or False: DALL-E requires detailed textual descriptions to generate images.
3. True or False: AI-driven design tools are only suitable for professional designers with extensive experience.

4. True or False: Amper Music allows users to create music without any prior musical knowledge.
5. True or False: AI video editing tools require advanced manual adjustments to enhance video content.

Answers:

1. False, 2. True, 3. False, 4. True, 5. False

Reflecting on this chapter, it's evident that AI's impact on creativity is profound and multifaceted. It simplifies tasks while expanding the horizons of what's possible in art, writing, and multimedia creation. By integrating these tools into your workflow, you gain both efficiency and a partner in innovation, encouraging you to push beyond traditional boundaries.

As we transition into the next chapter, we will explore the ethical considerations of using AI in creative fields. We'll delve into how responsible usage ensures that this powerful technology enhances human creativity without compromising authenticity or integrity. Stay tuned as we unravel AI's potential to transform how we create and think about creation.

8

DATA PRIVACY AND ETHICS IN AI

> *"The pace of progress in artificial intelligence is incredibly fast... The risk of something seriously dangerous happening is in the five-year time frame."*
>
> — ELON MUSK

UNDERSTANDING AI'S ETHICAL IMPLICATIONS

One evening a couple of years back, I found myself in a lively discussion with friends about AI's growing role in our lives. We debated whether the convenience AI offers is worth the trade-off in privacy. It struck me then how crucial it is to consider the ethics behind these powerful tools. Many people are unwilling to share their personal data with AI applications, even though AI systems thrive on data. Applications cannot be 100% accurate when they only have access to data from a portion of the population.

AI ethics is not just about creating intelligent machines—it's about ensuring these machines serve the greater good. Ethical AI demands that we scrutinize how algorithms can unintentionally harbor biases, influencing decisions from loan approvals to hiring practices. These biases often stem from unrepresentative data, leading to skewed outcomes that can perpetuate inequality.

Consider a scenario where AI systems calculate credit scores. If the training data heavily favors individuals from specific demo-graphics, it might inadvertently marginalize underrepresented groups, creating a barrier to financial access. A similar concern in recruitment is that algorithms scanning resumes might favor specific educational backgrounds, excluding candidates who might be more qualified. Failure to correct biases in AI will severely undermine its potential for unity.

AI's capacity to analyze massive volumes of transactional data raises serious concerns regarding user privacy and data security. Companies store and analyze every digital footprint you leave—search history, online purchases, even your location. While this data helps AI personalize experiences, it also risks infringing on your privacy and individual rights. The challenge emerges when AI systems make decisions that impact your life, such as eligibility for a service or product, with little transparency. This opacity can lead to unfair treatment and discrimination if unchecked.

To counteract this, initiatives focused on developing AI with built-in transparency and fairness protocols are gaining traction. For example, incorporating checks that ensure data used in AI models is diverse and representative is the best way forward. Platforms where users can see and understand AI systems' data trails and decision logic reduce mistrust.

Besides the challenges of bias and privacy, AI systems also present ethical concerns in terms of accountability and responsibility. Who bears the blame when AI makes a decision that leads to a negative outcome, such as the incorrect denial of a service or an allocation of invested funds that delivers substandard returns? As AI systems see increased use in high-stakes environments like healthcare and law enforcement, the questions become more complex. Ensuring that AI's decision-making processes are transparent and accountable is paramount for ethical implementation.

In healthcare, for example, AI is able to learn to diagnose diseases, but the stakes are high if a wrong diagnosis arises due to algorithmic flaws. Developers and healthcare providers must collaborate to fine-tune these systems, ensuring they operate within set ethical guidelines and can be audited for accountability. Similarly, in law enforcement, AI tools must be transparent enough for stakeholders to understand their workings and outcomes, facilitating trust.

Ethical concerns surrounding AI extend beyond bias and privacy. As AI systems grow in sophistication, they threaten to replace human jobs, raising fundamental questions about workforce evolution. This shift necessitates balancing innovation and job security, as automation will displace workers in various industries. A forward-looking approach requires retraining and upskilling programs to help the existing workforce transition to new roles emphasizing human skills like emotional intelligence and creativity. Meanwhile, the responsibility lies equally with developers and users to ensure the ethical deployment of AI. Developers must prioritize transparency and fairness, embedding ethical standards within AI frameworks from the start. Users should remain vigilant, questioning how AI tools influence decisions and demanding transparent systems.

Promoting fairness and transparency in AI applications is vital for fostering trust and accountability. When you use an AI tool, understanding its decision-making process should be straightforward. Lack of clarity often leads to mistrust, which is why explainable AI is essential. Systems should offer clear documentation and visualization tools that demystify their operations. For developers, explainability means incorporating features that allow users to understand how algorithms reach their outcomes. By employing transparency and simplifying the complexity inside AI systems, we enable broader access and involvement in AI technology, reducing the divide between knowledgeable experts and everyday users.

Numerous resources offer guidance and support for those eager to delve deeper into ethical AI practices. Organizations like UNESCO provide frameworks for ethical AI development, advocating for human rights-centered approaches. Publications from industry leaders present guidelines on responsible AI use, encouraging stakeholders to engage in ongoing dialogue about ethics. By leveraging these resources, you can contribute to a culture of ethical awareness in AI deployment. Ethical literacy in AI doesn't just rest on developers; it involves every stakeholder, from users to policymakers, ensuring that AI technologies continue to benefit society broadly.

Reader's Resources: Ethical AI Resource List

- **UNESCO Recommendation on the Ethics of Artificial Intelligence**: A global standard for ethical AI practices, assisting countries in formulating policies that protect human and civil rights in the age of AI.

- **IBM's AI Privacy Insights**: Guidance on navigating privacy issues in AI, offering practical steps to uphold data ethics in product development.
- **Atlassian's Responsible AI Blog**: Discusses principles and best practices for ethical AI development, providing case studies and examples from various industries.

Interaction with these resources equips you with the knowledge to navigate the ethical landscape of AI confidently. As we advance technologically, maintaining this ethical compass ensures that AI remains a force for good in society. It is through informed awareness and proactive engagement that AI can be aligned with the values we cherish as a society, using technology as a tool for justice and equity.

SAFEGUARDING YOUR DATA WHEN USING AI

Let's talk about data privacy. It's the backbone of any digital interaction today, especially with AI. Imagine your personal information—a mosaic of details like your location, shopping habits, or even health data—being collected and stored. AI tools often gather this data to tailor experiences, making them more intuitive and relevant. However, the stakes are high if this data lands in the wrong hands. Data breaches are typically executed to enable identity theft, financial fraud, and invasion of privacy. The consequences are real, and understanding these risks is crucial for anyone using AI technology.

AI tools typically collect a range of data types. This includes basic information like your name and email address but can also extend to more sensitive details like your biometric data or browsing history. These pieces help refine AI algorithms, enabling them to predict your needs or preferences with uncanny accuracy. However, this level of access demands informed consent. You should know what data is being collected, why it's needed, and how it will be used. Without this transparency, using AI becomes a game of blind trust.

Securing your data doesn't require complex strategies; it involves smart practices. Start by using encryption to protect data during transmission. Encryption transforms your data into an unreadable format that can only be accessed with a key, adding a layer of security against unauthorized access. Always configure privacy settings in AI applications to limit the data you share. Many apps allow you to control what information they collect and store. Adjust these settings to enhance your privacy without sacrificing functionality.

AI plays a dual role in data privacy—it can act as both a protector and a challenger. On one side, AI-driven cybersecurity solutions are formidable allies in threat detection and response. They can identify unusual patterns in network traffic, flagging potential cyber threats before they escalate. Conversely, AI's capacity to process vast amounts of data can also be a privacy concern. If not handled correctly, AI could inadvertently expose, or misuse personal information stored within its systems.

Mitigating these risks involves technical solutions and cultivating a culture of privacy awareness. Users must be educated about the value of their data and the implications of sharing it. Workshops, online courses, and seminars can provide valuable insights into best practices for data protection, encouraging a proactive stance on privacy. Organizations must also foster environments where privacy is prioritized, setting an example and empowering users to take control of their digital footprints.

To build on this, consider scenarios where data privacy failures led to significant consequences—whether through avoidable breaches or unintentional mishandling of data. Reviewing case studies where strict privacy protocols prevented or minimized damage can offer important lessons. To ensure consistent adherence to standardized privacy measures, organizations should regularly conduct audits and compliance checks.

Maintaining privacy requires vigilance and proactive measures. One crucial step is reviewing the terms of service and privacy policies for any AI tool you use. These documents outline how your data will be managed, giving you insight into potential risks. Performing regular software updates is another key strategy to patch vulnerabilities that hackers might exploit. Updates often include security enhancements that protect against new threats, so staying current reduces risk exposure.

Let's consider some practical tips for data privacy. First, minimize the personal information you share online. The less data you provide, the less there is to compromise. Another strategy is using strong, unique passwords for different platforms. This limits the damage a single data breach can cause across your accounts. Additionally, two-factor authentication should be enabled for an extra security layer. Finally, consider using a virtual private network (VPN) whenever you are connected to the internet. You can also use privacy-focused web browsers like Brave and Firefox, along with search engines that emphasize user confidentiality rather than data collection.

Thinking about data privacy isn't just about preventing potential threats; it's about empowering yourself with knowledge and control over your digital footprint. These steps protect your personal information and assert your right to privacy in an increasingly connected world. In a broader scope, advocating for stricter privacy regulations and actively participating in discussions about data ethics represent crucial parts of safeguarding our digital futures collectively.

Reader's Resource: Data Privacy Checklist

- Use encryption tools for secure data transmission.
- Regularly review and adjust app privacy settings.
- Stay informed by reading the terms of service.
- Keep software up to date for security patches.
- Employ strong passwords and two-factor authentication.

This checklist serves as a guide to help safeguard your personal information while maximizing AI's benefits without compromising your privacy. By taking these steps, we move closer to a safer, more transparent digital ecosystem where individuals retain agency over their data and digital identities.

RESPONSIBLE AI PRACTICES

Imagine a world where AI is not only a tool but a responsible partner in our daily lives. Responsible AI is not just a lofty ideal. It is now necessary for personal and professional landscapes. Embracing ethical AI practices means more than just avoiding harm; it's about fostering transparency and accountability in every interaction. Transparency ensures that AI systems are understandable and their decisions traceable. Accountability demands that those who design and deploy AI are answerable for its outcomes. This approach builds a foundation of trust between technology and its users, which is crucial in today's interconnected world.

One of the biggest challenges in AI development is ensuring diversity and inclusivity. An AI system is only as unbiased as the data it's fed. If the datasets lack diversity, the AI's decisions will probably reflect these blind spots, perpetuating stereotypes and potentially causing harm. By incorporating diverse perspectives into AI development, we can create systems that better reflect the society they serve. This means involving people from various backgrounds in the design process, ensuring the technology we build doesn't inadvertently marginalize any group.

Implementing responsible AI practices requires action. Start by conducting bias audits on AI algorithms. These audits help identify and mitigate any biases before they cause real-world issues. Fairness checks can be integrated into AI systems to ensure they operate equitably across different demographics. Regular reviews of AI outputs can pinpoint discrepancies, allowing for timely corrections. By embedding fairness into the fabric of AI systems, we promote equality and justice in their applications.

The benefits of responsible AI use extend beyond technical correctness; they foster trust and credibility with stakeholders. When people know that an organization prioritizes ethical AI use, it enhances its reputation and strengthens relationships with clients, partners, and the community. Moreover, by addressing ethical concerns proactively, businesses reduce the risk of legal troubles or public backlash. This foresight protects both the company and its users, creating a safer environment for innovation.

Consider how a multinational corporation integrating responsible AI practices into its operations becomes more resilient. Suppose this company exhibits transparency by routinely publishing its data auditing practices and outcomes. In that case, it adheres to regulatory standards and builds trust among customers and regulatory bodies.

Numerous resources are available to support responsible AI implementation. Many leading organizations offer AI ethics toolkits and frameworks designed to guide ethical practices. These tools provide actionable insights into developing transparent, accountable AI systems. Case studies from companies successfully implementing ethical AI offer valuable lessons and inspire confidence in new adopters. By studying these examples, you can learn practical strategies for navigating the ethical landscape of AI use.

Reader's Resources: Responsible AI Ethics Resources List

- **AI Ethics Toolkits**: Comprehensive guides from leading organizations offering frameworks for embedding ethics in AI development processes, emphasizing accountability.
- **Case Studies**: Examples of successful ethical AI implementation provide hands-on guidance and lessons for organizations and developers.
- **Frameworks**: Structured approaches to ensure that AI systems are designed and applied in ways that consider the societal impacts and ethical implications.

These resources serve as a compass, helping you navigate the complex terrain of ethical AI practices with confidence and clarity. As we continue integrating AI into our lives, maintaining this ethical framework ensures that advancements are available to everyone.

Responsible AI is no longer merely a topic for tech experts—it's a call to action for anyone using these technologies. By understanding its principles and applying them thoughtfully, we all contribute to a future where technology enhances life without compromising ethics or integrity. The inclusion of AI literacy in education systems will prepare future generations to engage critically with these technologies and to advocate effectively for continuous improvement in AI standards.

BALANCING AI BENEFITS WITH ETHICAL CONCERNS

Imagine waking up to an AI-enabled seamless morning routine; a world with AI-optimized schedules and timely reminders, all because of the tech at your fingertips. AI's most enticing promise is the potential to enhance life quality and productivity. However, there's another side to this shiny coin. We cannot ignore AI's growing impact on employment. Automation, while boosting efficiency, might lead to job displacement in specific sectors. The challenge is ensuring that society adapts to these changes and supports workers transitioning to new roles while embracing technological advancements.

Ethical considerations in AI use are not just a box to check—they're integral to sustainable innovation. As we develop and deploy AI, understanding its long-term consequences is crucial. Every algorithm and decision these systems make can ripple outwards, affecting real lives and communities. Ethics must guide us in balancing innovation with responsibility. Developers must embed ethical principles into AI design, ensuring systems serve humanity positively rather than exacerbate existing inequalities. This balance helps prevent unintended harm and builds systems that reflect shared values.

Consider the case of autonomous vehicles—while they promise revolutionary changes in transportation, the societal implications are vast. From altering urban landscapes to affecting employment for those in driving professions, the impacts require strategic planning and ethical foresight. Industry stakeholders, therefore, play a crucial role in ensuring that such transformations are inclusive and beneficial to society.

The ethical implications of AI tools should be considered before diving in. It's about asking the right questions: Does this tool respect user privacy? Is it designed with fairness in mind? Engage in discussions about ethics within your professional circles, encouraging a culture of accountability. These conversations can lead to better practices and heightened awareness. It's about being proactive; recognizing potential pitfalls and addressing them head-on ensures AI's benefits are maximized without compromising integrity or trust.

There are inspiring examples of ethical AI practices worth noting in the real world. Note that some companies prioritize transparency, giving users insights into data usage and protection. Other organizations implement rigorous testing to identify and mitigate bias, ensuring their products operate equitably across diverse user groups. Others invest in community engagement, seeking feedback from those impacted by AI decisions to refine their approach. These actions demonstrate a commitment to responsible AI use, illustrating how ethics can coexist with technological progress.

Sustainable solutions in AI ethics involve interdisciplinary collaboration, where technologists, ethicists, sociologists, and policymakers work together to create comprehensive guidelines and policies. Considering multiple perspectives can bridge the gap between innovative capacities and ethical responsibilities, ensuring that AI's trajectory aligns with societal well-being.

Chapter 8 Reader Quiz

As we wrap up the in-depth exploration of AI's ethical and privacy considerations, it's time to reflect and test your understanding. This isn't just about getting the correct answers; it's about ensuring you grasp the essence of these critical topics. Let's see what you have gleaned from the discussion on data privacy, ethical AI practices, and balancing benefits with concerns.

1. What role does transparency play in responsible AI practices?

A. It complicates the development process
B. It ensures AI systems are understandable, and decisions are traceable
C. It focuses solely on improving AI speed
D. It allows for unchecked innovation

2. Which of the following best describes the dual nature of AI's impact?

A. It only improves productivity
B. It enhances quality of life while posing risks like job displacement
C. It focuses solely on data privacy issues
D. It guarantees job security for all

3. How can individuals contribute to ethical AI use?

A. By ignoring ethical guidelines
B. By engaging in discussions and evaluating tools for fairness
C. By using AI without considering its implications
D. By leaving all decisions to developers

4. What is a key benefit of responsible AI use for businesses?

A. It reduces transparency requirements
B. It builds trust and credibility with stakeholders
C. It allows for the unchecked collection of data
D. It eliminates the need for legal compliance.

5. Which strategy helps safeguard data privacy when using AI tools?

A. Only using outdated software versions
B. Regularly updating software and reviewing privacy settings
C. Sharing all personal information freely
D. Avoiding encryption for ease of access.

Answers: 1-B, 2-B, 3-B, 4-B, 5-B

As we conclude this chapter, we've delved into the complex interplay between AI ethics, data privacy, and responsible usage. These elements are not theoretical but practical and crucial for anyone engaging with AI today. Understanding them helps you navigate this technology's landscape with confidence and foresight. AI holds immense potential to transform lives, but it requires careful consideration of ethical implications and privacy concerns.

This chapter aimed to equip you with knowledge and strategies to engage with AI responsibly and thoughtfully. As we move forward, we'll explore how these principles apply in various fields, ensuring that technology serves humanity in positive ways. Stay curious and considerate as we continue this exploration into AI. Our journey underscores the importance of ethical vigilance, promising a future where AI enhances our world without compromising its foundations.

9
INTERACTIVE AI LEARNING

"AI can bring academic subjects to life, serve as a Socratic tutor, and allow for personalized education at individual paces."

— SAL KHAN, FOUNDER OF KHAN ACADEMY

TEST YOUR KNOWLEDGE WITH AI QUIZZES

As you sip your morning coffee, you decide to challenge yourself with a quick AI quiz. It feels like a game, but every question is a step toward mastering AI concepts. Quizzes transform your learning experience from passive reading to active participation. Imagine testing your understanding of foundational AI terms and seeing instant feedback. These quizzes help you differentiate between AI, machine learning, and deep learning, ensuring you remember these concepts. It is crucial to understand these distinctions as they each play unique roles in technology's landscape.

For instance, you might encounter questions that ask you to match terms like "supervised learning" with its definition or identify scenarios where "deep learning" excels over other forms. These quizzes serve as checkpoints, reinforcing your knowledge while highlighting areas needing further exploration. They can also include real-world scenarios, like identifying AI applications in everyday gadgets or services. This reflection pushes you beyond rote memorization, inviting you into a space where theoretical knowledge meets practical applications.

Reader's Resource: Quizzes on AI Topics.

There are several online sources for quizzes on AI topics. These can be categorized as Educational Platforms, Quiz & Trivia websites, and Tech and Developer Sites for advanced topics. Specific examples include:

Educational Platforms

1. **Coursera (**https://www.coursera.org) offers over 100 AI courses with built-in quizzes.
2. **edX (**https://www.edx.org**)** offers quizzes within courses from Harvard, MIT, and others. Topics include machine learning, ethics, robotics, and more.
3. **Kaggle** (https://www.kaggle.com/learn) offers hands-on AI mini-courses with embedded quizzes.

Quiz & Trivia Websites

1. **ProProfs Quiz** (https://www.proprofs.com/quiz-school) has dozens of quiz options in its Artificial Intelligence section.
2. **Quizizz** (https://quizizz.com) provides Interactive quizzes on AI concepts for all levels.

3. **Toppr / Byju's** (https://www.toppr.com) offers AI and computer science quizzes for high school and early college levels.

Tech and Developer Sites

1. **GeeksforGeeks** (https://www.geeksforgeeks.org) provides practice quizzes on AI, ML, and deep learning that are excellent for technical interview prep.
2. **W3Schools Machine Learning Section (**https://www.w3schools.com) has short quizzes on various AI/ML topics.
3. **TutorialsPoint (**https://www.tutorialspoint.com/artificial_intelligences) offers quick multiple-choice quizzes after short AI tutorials.

Interactive learning transforms education from passive information absorption into active application of knowledge in real-world contexts. For example, AI-powered quizzes can prompt learners to consider how smart home devices function and adapt, encouraging a more profound understanding of everyday technology. This approach fosters critical thinking and innovation, enabling students to engage with material in a meaningful way. This is not just learning; it's training your brain to think in an additional dimension of possibility and innovation. The quizzes don't just test; they teach. You gain deeper insights when you review your answers, especially the incorrect ones. Many times, understanding why an answer was wrong is often more enlightening than getting it right by chance.

A real-world example of AI's benefits to education is the use of ChatGPT and Bing Chat in STEM education. These AI tools serve as "objects-to-think-with," helping students develop reflective and critical thinking skills by engaging in simulated learning experiences. Such interactions promote creativity, problem-solving, and concept comprehension, illustrating the potential of AI to enhance educational outcomes.

Self-quizzing encourages continuous improvement, urging you to revisit materials and strengthen weak points. Self-assessment helps create a tailored learning journey, allowing you to focus on topics where you are less confident. It's about building a durable foundation, ensuring you don't just skim the surface but genuinely comprehend each concept. Regular self-assessment keeps you engaged and aware of your progress, providing a sense of accomplishment with every quiz completed. Embrace this practice to improve your understanding and retention of AI concepts. It's like having a personal tutor who guides you through each chapter, ensuring you are on track and motivated to keep pushing boundaries.

Effective learning by quizzing completion demands setting a strategy. Set aside some of your AI learning time for taking quizzes, treating it as an integral part of your learning routine rather than an afterthought. Analyze mistakes without haste—each error is an opportunity to deepen your understanding. Consider creating a study group or discussion forum where quiz results can spark conversations and collective learning. Sharing insights and diverse perspectives enriches the experience, providing new angles on complex topics.

To maximize learning from quizzes, approach them as tools to enhance comprehension, not as exams to pass or fail. Focus on the journey rather than the destination. By prioritizing understanding over scores, you embrace a growth mindset that celebrates progress and persistence.

Interactive Element: Quiz Reflection Journal

Start a journal where you jot down reflections after each quiz session. Note which questions challenged you, what patterns emerge in your answers, and how your understanding evolves. This practice fosters a deeper connection with the material and provides a tangible record of your progress. By documenting this journey, you can trace your development, recognize recurring challenges, and target specific areas for improvement, ultimately crafting a personalized roadmap to mastery.

Additionally, reviewing your journal regularly can provide motivational insights. Seeing how far you have come can inspire a positive mindset and a renewed commitment to your AI studies. As your journal grows, you may note improvements in your quiz scores, revealing how your understanding has deepened. This continuity and visibility of progress further fuel your enthusiasm and determination to conquer more challenging AI topics.

Incorporating quizzes into your study routine can transform your AI learning experience. They offer immediate feedback, helping you identify strengths and areas for improvement. By engaging actively with the material, you learn about AI and become part of its ever-evolving narrative. Quizzes are more than just questions—they are milestones on your path to AI proficiency.

HANDS-ON EXERCISES FOR PRACTICAL AI SKILLS

Imagine your satisfaction from creating something tangible with AI. Hands-on exercises provide this opportunity, turning abstract concepts into practical skills. By rolling up your sleeves and diving into mini projects, you engage actively with AI, enhancing understanding and retention. This isn't just about reading; it's about doing. Designing simple projects lets you apply what you have learned in tangible ways, allowing you to see theories come to life. For instance, creating simple AI models through platforms like Teachable Machine enables you to experiment without extensive programming knowledge. These projects serve as a playground for innovation, letting you explore how AI can solve actual problems.

These exercises are not difficult to prepare. Start by selecting tools that match your skill level and project goals. Teachable Machine offers an intuitive interface to build models by uploading images or sounds. It guides you through the process, making it accessible even for beginners. In a similar manner, Google Colab provides a platform to conduct data experiments leveraging Python's power without the hassle of local installation. It's a cloud-based service that supports collaborative coding, which is ideal for running data experiments or testing algorithms. By following detailed guides, you can set up exercises that build competence and confidence in handling AI tasks.

Hands-on learning holds immense benefits. The use of theoretical knowledge in practical scenarios solidifies concepts that might otherwise remain abstract. Successfully completing a project boosts confidence, showing that you can navigate the complexities of AI. This experiential learning approach is invaluable. It transforms passive reading into active problem-solving, bridging the gap between theory and real-world application. Each project completed is a step forward in your AI journey, reinforcing knowledge and building new skills simultaneously.

Maximizing these learning opportunities requires a strategic approach. Interaction with peers can enrich the experience, providing diverse perspectives and feedback that enhance understanding. Group projects facilitate shared learning and collective problem-solving, making complex concepts more digestible. Iteration is another key strategy; revisiting projects to refine skills and techniques leads to mastery. You deepen your understanding and increase your proficiency by continuously improving your models or solutions. This iterative process encourages exploration and innovation, pushing the boundaries of what you thought possible.

It is crucial to approach hands-on exercises with curiosity and an open mind. View each task as a chance to discover something new about AI and yourself. Experiment freely; don't shy away from mistakes—they're part of learning. Every error teaches you how to improve, bringing you closer to mastering AI's potential. Engage with exercise materials thoroughly, questioning each step and seeking to understand the underlying logic. This critical engagement fosters deeper insights and better retention.

To illustrate the power of iterative experimentation, consider a scenario where you develop a predictive model. Initially, you may focus on grasping the basics—inputting data, understanding parameters, and receiving output. As you proceed, fine-tuning the model becomes an enriching exercise. Your familiarity with AI tools grows with each adjustment, equipping you with the skill set to explore even more sophisticated applications.

Engage actively and explore the diverse tools at your disposal. Coursera and edX offer excellent AI courses that help you understand concepts better, while GitHub hosts code repositories for various AI projects. Websites like Kaggle allow you to participate in data science competitions to test your skills against your peers. These platforms broaden the scope of learning while providing practical insight into AI applications.

So, dive into these exercises as opportunities for growth and exploration in the vast field of AI. Embrace the challenges and celebrate the victories, no matter how small they may seem. Each completed exercise adds a new tool to your AI toolkit, preparing you for more complex challenges.

REAL-WORLD AI CHALLENGES: CAN YOU SOLVE THEM?

One area where AI skills come to life is analyzing customer feedback with sentiment analysis. It's about extracting emotions from text to understand how people feel about a product or service. Picture a tool that sifts through thousands of comments, identifying patterns in customer satisfaction or discontent. This task requires you to pinpoint objectives and constraints—like focusing on specific sentiment keywords—and break it down into manageable steps. You might start by selecting a dataset and then choosing an AI tool capable of processing natural language. Creation of a plan requires establishing clear milestones, maintaining a logical progression, and making necessary modifications. It's not just about the technical side; it's about creativity and experimentation.

Consider the challenge of creating a chatbot for customer service automation. Think of it as crafting a virtual assistant that can handle inquiries around the clock. Start by defining the scope—what frequent questions should it address? Break tasks into smaller parts: designing conversation flows, integrating the bot with existing systems, and testing responses. A step-by-step plan ensures you cover all bases, from initial set-up to deployment. This process encourages creative problem-solving, urging you to test different approaches and iterate based on feedback.

Another thrilling challenge is analyzing social media trends for marketing insights. Social platforms overflow with data waiting to be harnessed. Your task might involve tracking trending topics and hashtags to inform marketing strategies. Begin by identifying key metrics—engagement rates, follower growth, or sentiment analysis. These insights can guide content creation and campaign adjustments. Each step sharpens your problem-solving skills, preparing you to tackle even more complex tasks as you gain confidence in applying AI knowledge.

Moreover, technology continuously evolves, presenting new avenues and resources to explore. Consider digital tools like APIs, which facilitate integration with other systems, or open-source platforms providing robust datasets. They offer a wealth of opportunities to apply your theoretical knowledge in a spectrum of scenarios—from enhancing user experience in digital applications to optimizing supply chain operations. This array of options encourages you to expand your AI skill set while staying informed about industry trends.

When roadblocks arise, collaboration offers fresh perspectives and solutions. Engage with peers to brainstorm ideas and share experiences—collective wisdom often leads to breakthroughs. Online resources and AI communities provide additional support, offering a treasure trove of information and guidance. Access forums or networks where enthusiasts gather to exchange knowledge. Sharing insights fosters a sense of camaraderie and accelerates learning.

Consider the example of a team optimizing supply chain logistics using AI. They employed machine learning algorithms to predict demand and streamline inventory management. Through teamwork and iterative refinement, they achieved remarkable efficiency gains, reducing waste and improving customer satisfaction (Intellias). Another inspiring example is a student who developed an AI-driven app for personalized learning, tailoring educational content based on user preferences and performance (Forbes Technology Council). These successes demonstrate the dramatic power of applying AI to real-world challenges.

Further opportunities emerge when diving deeper into the domains of finance, healthcare, and environmental science. For instance, AI applications in finance involve developing algorithms to predict market trends, while in healthcare, they aid in patient diagnosis and personalized medicine initiatives. These fields, brimming with potential and complexity, benefit immensely from AI's innovative solutions.

By engaging with these challenges, you refine your skills and discover new applications for AI in diverse fields. This hands-on experience prepares you for future endeavors, equipping you with the tools and confidence to tackle increasingly intricate problems. Embrace the opportunity to explore AI's potential and unlock new possibilities through creativity and collaboration.

BUILDING CONFIDENCE: SMALL WINS WITH AI

In AI learning, minor achievements are building blocks of confidence and motivation. Picture the satisfaction from completing your first AI-driven task, like automating a repetitive chore with a simple script. This modest accomplishment can ignite a spark, compelling you to explore further. Celebrating these moments reinforces the notion that progress is tangible and within reach. Recognizing each step forward, no matter how small, shifts your perspective from focusing on the end goal to appreciating the learning process. This mindset change can lead to sustained motivation, keeping you engaged even when the going gets tough.

Setting manageable goals is key to achieving these small wins. Begin by identifying short-term objectives that align with your broader learning aspirations. For instance, if you are interested in natural language processing, start by coding a basic sentiment analysis tool. Track your progress diligently, noting each milestone reached. This could be as simple as successfully installing a software package or debugging a tricky line of code. By breaking down larger tasks into smaller, achievable parts, you create a roadmap that guides you steadily toward your ultimate goal. Each tick on this roadmap serves as a reminder of your progress, boosting your confidence and encouraging further exploration.

The benefits of these small wins extend beyond immediate gratification. They lay the groundwork for tackling more complex challenges down the line. Each success builds a scaffold of confidence, bolstering your belief in your capability to conquer intricate AI problems later. This foundational confidence is crucial when you encounter setbacks or daunting tasks. It reminds you that you have overcome obstacles and can do so again. Moreover, these incremental successes keep your motivation levels high, making the learning process enjoyable and rewarding rather than overwhelming and daunting.

Consider the story of Sam, a high school student who decided to explore AI by creating a chatbot for his school project. Initially intimidated by the technicalities, Sam set a modest goal: designing a bot that could answer basic FAQs about his school. He started small, focusing on crafting simple response patterns. As he saw his bot come to life, his confidence grew. This small win encouraged Sam to expand the bot's capabilities, eventually integrating it with his school's website. This journey enhanced his technical skills and boosted his self-esteem, proving that small steps can lead to significant achievements.

Another example is Alex, a marketing professional who dabbled in AI to optimize social media strategies. Instead of attempting to overhaul entire campaigns simultaneously, Alex focused on using AI tools to schedule posts more efficiently. Alex improved his team's productivity and results by analyzing optimal posting times and content engagement metrics. This success motivated him to delve deeper into AI analytics, leading to more sophisticated marketing strategies over time. These stories underscore the power of starting small and building upon each success.

While learning about AI, embracing small wins will redefine your educational experience. It transforms potential frustration into motivation, turning every completed task into a starting point for future endeavors. By focusing on achievable goals and celebrating progress, you cultivate an environment where confidence thrives and curiosity flourishes. This approach enhances your skills and fosters a lifelong love for learning, ensuring your AI exploration remains fruitful and fulfilling.

By engaging in new AI challenges and projects, you are developing a robust skill set and a resilient mindset. This resilience is vital when dealing with complex problems, as it underscores the role of every victory in advancing towards AI mastery.

As you reach the end of this chapter, it's time to challenge your understanding and see how much you have absorbed. This quiz will test your knowledge and reinforce the concepts we've explored while helping identify areas needing more attention.

Chapter 9 Reader Quiz

1. What distinguishes machine learning from deep learning?

A. Deep learning uses neural networks
B. Machine learning is more complex
C. Both are identical
D. Machine learning requires no data.

2. Which term refers to AI systems' ability to improve from experience?

A. Static processing,
B. Machine learning,
C. Manual coding, or
D. Data deletion

3. How can AI enhance daily productivity?

A. A) By replacing all human tasks
B. B) Through automation of repetitive tasks
C. C) By increasing workload
D. D) By eliminating technology use

4. What is the benefit of regular self-assessment in learning?

A. Promotes stagnation
B. Identifies knowledge gaps
C. Guarantees immediate expertise
D. Discourages further study

Answers:

1-A, 2-B, 3-B, 4-B

Summary

In this chapter, we navigated through the dynamic world of interactive AI learning, where quizzes, hands-on exercises, real-world challenges, and small wins play pivotal roles. By actively engaging with these elements, you pave the way for deeper comprehension and practical skills that transcend theoretical knowledge. The next chapter will explore AI's role in specific industries and how these tools can revolutionize different fields. Whether transforming healthcare, advancing retail, or innovating within the automotive industry, your AI journey is poised for remarkable growth and discovery.

10
REWIND: REAL-WORLD AI SUCCESS STORIES

"AI will perform tasks requiring specialized skills, making great medical advice and tutoring free and commonplace."

— BILL GATES

GROUNDBREAKING AI IN HEALTHCARE

Imagine a world where the nuances of human health are illuminated through the precision of AI, unveiling early hints of diseases before they manifest into noticeable ailments. This extraordinary ability of artificial intelligence is rapidly transforming healthcare, morphing once distant dreams into today's realities. Today, AI has become a core aspect of medical practices, enhancing the precision and efficiency of patient care through cutting-edge tools.

CASE STUDY—FETAL MONITORING BY AI

At the Area 25 Health Centre in Lilongwe, Malawi, AI-enabled fetal monitoring software has been implemented to reduce stillbirths and neonatal deaths. This technology continuously monitors a baby's vital signs in real time during labor, allowing clinicians to detect and respond to complications in real time. Since its introduction, the center has reported an 82% reduction in stillbirths and neonatal deaths, highlighting the significant impact of AI in improving maternal and neonatal outcomes in resource-limited settings.

AI tools allow healthcare professionals to identify health concerns long before they materialize, scrutinizing extensive datasets to uncover patterns that might escape even the most skilled human eye. This offers predictive diagnostic accuracy that was once deemed unattainable. In bustling hospitals, AI-powered predictive analytics impact resource allocation, meticulously ensuring that staff and equipment are optimally deployed where needed. This innovation not only streamlines efficiency but substantially improves patient outcomes by reducing wait times and refining the delivery of care.

For instance, using AI to create personalized treatment plans for cancer demonstrates AI's breakthrough capabilities. Sophisticated algorithms delve into genetic data, crafting tailored treatment regimens that heighten success rates while minimizing adverse side effects. Such precision medicine perfectly exemplifies AI's dramatic impact on healthcare.

Artificial intelligence (AI) revolutionizes diagnostic practices by enhancing accuracy and efficiency. AI algorithms, particularly in radiology, adeptly analyze complex scans to detect abnormalities that might elude the human eye, serving as reliable secondary reviewers. This collaboration between AI and healthcare professionals accelerates diagnosis, minimizes human error, and facilitates timely interventions.

Functioning like a meticulous digital assistant, AI processes vast amounts of imaging data with remarkable precision, enabling clinicians to focus more on patient care. This interplay improves diagnostic outcomes and alleviates the workload on medical staff, addressing challenges such as burnout and resource constraints. As AI continues to integrate into healthcare systems, it empowers medical professionals to achieve levels of diagnostic capability previously unattainable.

Patient care is further bolstered by AI chatbots that handle patient inquiries and schedule appointments. This frees medical personnel to concentrate on more pressing tasks and ensures patients receive timely and accurate responses. Meanwhile, virtual health assistants monitor patients' health remotely, vigilantly tracking vital signs and alerting healthcare providers at the first sign of irregularities. This convergence of human expertise and AI technology enhances patient outcomes and elevates their experience by providing continuous, personalized care, all while reducing the need for frequent hospital visits.

CASE STUDY—AI-ASSISTED ROBOTIC SURGERY

Maastricht University Medical Center in the Netherlands uses AI-assisted robotic systems to perform highly precise surgical procedures. Surgeons have employed these systems to suture extremely narrow blood vessels measuring between 0.03 and 0.08 millimeters in diameter. The integration of AI with robotic surgery enhances precision, reduces variability in surgical outcomes, and allows for minimally invasive procedures that were previously challenging or impossible with traditional techniques.

The use of AI in healthcare transcends mere technological advancement; it substantially reimagines the entire care delivery. It uses sophisticated algorithms to complement human expertise, ensuring superior patient outcomes and more personalized care experiences. As AI technologies evolve, the scope for further innovation within healthcare remains expansive and promising, offering pathways to even more tailored and effective medical interventions.

AI INNOVATIONS IN RETAIL AND E-COMMERCE

Imagine stepping into a store where every suggestion feels utterly bespoke just for you. AI's profound impact on the industry brings this personalized retail experience to life. Retailers harness AI-driven recommendations to craft unique shopping experiences that enhance consumer satisfaction and boost sales. By strategically analyzing past purchases, browsing history, and social media activity, AI algorithms discern shopping patterns and suggest products that align seamlessly with individual preferences.

For example, Sephora's Virtual Artist is an AI-powered app that allows customers to try on makeup virtually using their phone's camera. This personalized experience increases product engagement and helps customers find the perfect shade. AI-driven retailing offers the sensation of having a personal shopper who intimately knows your tastes, transforming shopping from a mundane task into an exciting journey tailored to the individual's desires.

Inventory management is another area where AI applications provide significant benefit in retail. Advanced algorithms enable optimal stock maintenance, ensuring that popular products remain readily available while avoiding overstocking less in-demand items. By leveraging demand forecasts derived from historical sales data, retailers can more precisely anticipate future needs, streamlining supply chains and reducing storage costs and wastage. AI enhances operational efficiency for retailers and consumers—a genuine win-win situation.

Implementing AI in retail might seem daunting to some, but it remains more accessible than anticipated. The journey begins by identifying areas within a business where AI can demonstrate its value. Leveraging AI for demand forecasting is impactful, revolutionizing inventory management by aligning stock levels with predictive sales data. Moreover, integrating AI-driven chatbots into customer service platforms has streamlined support services, offering instantaneous responses to customer questions and resolving simple issues with minimal human intervention, thus providing a seamless customer experience.

Enhancing customer experience is critical to retail success, and AI plays a vital role in achieving this goal. AI-powered product recommendations transform shopping from a mundane activity into an engaging experience uniquely tailored to individual preferences. Chatbots tirelessly operate, available around the clock to assist with everything from product inquiries to issue resolution, enhancing customer satisfaction and fostering brand loyalty through personalized attention.

Success stories in retail illustrate AI's profound impact. A well-known retail chain adeptly uses AI in personalized marketing, crafting targeted advertisements and promotions that resonate deeply with individual consumers. This approach boosts sales and strengthens customer relationships by making interactions feel personal and meaningful. Similarly, e-commerce platforms have leveraged AI to optimize product recommendations, leading to enhanced user experiences and conversion rates.

The impact of AI on retail and e-commerce is undeniably positive. AI enhances efficiency, personalization, and overall customer satisfaction. As technology becomes more deeply integrated into operations, the industry's potential for innovation and growth remains boundless. Whether through personalized shopping experiences or optimized inventory systems, AI offers invaluable solutions benefiting retailers and consumers.

AI'S ROLE IN MODERN EDUCATION

AI is ushering in an educational transformation by reshaping how students engage with learning processes. Academic experiences are enriched by AI tools that personalize learning journeys. Picture a classroom where lessons adapt to each student's pace, providing challenges when needed. This is the progressive power of AI-driven personalized learning platforms. By analyzing student data, these platforms customize educational content, ensuring each learner receives the optimal level of complexity and learning assistance. AI empowers students to stay engaged, turning potential frustration into inquisitive pursuit.

Adaptive technologies add a layer of personalization, providing educational experiences catering to students' unique requirements. These technologies adeptly identify a student's strengths and areas for improvement, dynamically adjusting curricula. This automation fosters personalized educational pathways, replacing the traditional one-size-fits-all model with individualized learning journeys that promote confidence and growth. Imagine this as a personal tutor who precisely understands the areas where you excel and where you need more support.

The impact of AI on student learning is profound. AI creates an environment where learning paths are dynamically customized based on real-time feedback. These personalized pathways create interactive and responsive learning experiences where students actively participate, receiving immediate assessments that clearly delineate progress and areas needing attention. This continuous feedback loop fosters active learning environments where students engage meaningfully rather than passively absorbing information.

Duolingo, a widely used language-learning platform, is an example of AI's pivotal role in education. Duolingo employs AI algorithms to personalize lessons based on individual user performance. The platform begins with an initial assessment to gauge a learner's proficiency and then continuously adapts the difficulty and content of subsequent exercises in response to the user's progress. This adaptive learning approach ensures that each student receives a tailored educational experience. Duolingo exemplifies how technology can create a more personalized and effective learning environment by leveraging AI to adjust to learners' needs in real time.

Incorporating AI within educational contexts requires thoughtful strategies. Educators have AI tools to craft personalized learning experiences, adapting lessons to accommodate diverse student needs. AI-driven curriculum development aids teachers in curating lesson plans that dynamically adapt, offering pertinent content as students progress. This integration supports students and empowers teachers by providing insightful analyses of classroom dynamics, culminating in enhanced teaching effectiveness.

Real-world instances illustrate the transformative potential of AI in education. A university successfully harnessed AI for personalized tutoring and student support, demonstrating improved academic outcomes and satisfaction. By analyzing data, AI identifies areas where students struggle, offering just-in-time assistance that helps them conquer challenges in real time. Likewise, one visionary educator employs AI to create adaptive learning materials that evolve based on student feedback, enhancing student engagement and ensuring access to education that aligns with each student's learning style.

Beyond individual classrooms, AI fosters an educational environment where all students can excel regardless of starting points. This technology equips educators with unparalleled knowledge about their students' needs, adapting teaching methods to be more inclusive and effective. As AI continues to evolve, its role in education's future promises to expand, presenting innovative solutions that enhance the educational journey for both students and teachers.

The plethora of early AI success stories points to a future where AI integration in education is guaranteed. These narratives signal a movement toward personalized, data-driven learning that benefits everyone involved. Educational AI applications foretell a bright future where education becomes accessible, engaging, and impactful for students around the world.

AI IN FINANCE: CASE STUDIES AND OUTCOMES

Imagine, for a moment, a financial world traditionally seen as a labyrinth of numbers and complexities now invigorated by AI's precision and swiftness. The financial sector is undergoing a profound transformation as AI reshapes transactions, investments, and risk management methodologies. AI-driven fraud detection systems are at the forefront, scanning enormous datasets to uncover anomalies and suspicious activities. These systems adapt to the constantly evolving threat landscape, utilizing machine learning algorithms that serve as a robust safeguard against financial crime. The result is a secure environment for institutions and consumers, where transactions proceed securely and confidently.

Beyond enhancing security, AI also revolutionizes stock market investments with automated trading algorithms. These advanced algorithms sift through vast quantities of data, executing trades with unprecedented speed and efficiency, outperforming human capabilities. By analyzing market conditions and tendencies, these algorithms render split-second decisions that maximize returns while mitigating risks.

Conceptual Model of Algorithmic Trading

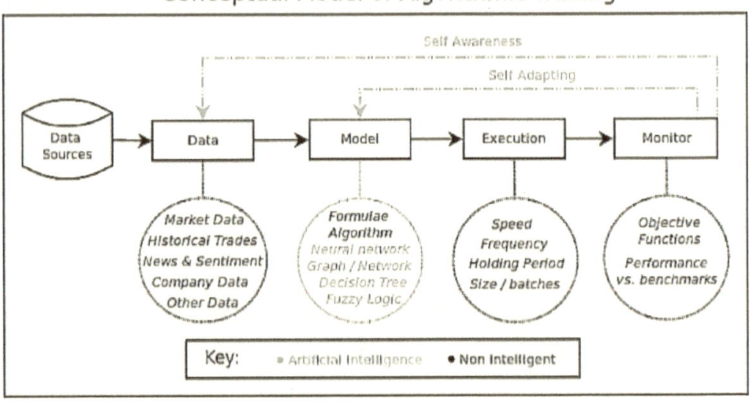

Consequently, AI levels the field between the previously elite world of sophisticated trading strategies and individual investors, empowering them to navigate the stock market landscape with newfound confidence.

AI's prowess in financial decision-making extends to enhancing investment strategies and risk management. AI-powered portfolio optimization tools analyze market data and adjust asset allocations in real time, ensuring portfolios align with investors' aspirations and risk tolerance. Predictive analytics impart foresight into market trends, enabling data-driven decisions to dominate investment strategies. This strategic edge boosts returns and diminishes risks, forging a more robust financial landscape.

For individual finance enthusiasts, AI offers comprehensive tools to simplify money management. Robo-advisors provide automated investment advice expertly tailored to personal preferences and ambitions. These platforms assess risk profiles, recommend diversified portfolios, and automatically rebalance investments to optimize performance. Similarly, AI-driven budgeting tools meticulously track spending habits, categorize expenses, and illuminate saving opportunities. This personalized approach empowers individuals to manage finances with heightened clarity and precision.

Countless success stories within the financial sector highlight institutions leveraging AI to their advantage. Consider, for instance, a national American bank that diminished fraudulent activities by over 50% within the first year by implementing AI-driven fraud detection. This milestone protects customer assets and savings and fosters trust in the bank's commitment to security. Similarly, hedge funds and currency traders employing AI algorithms dynamically adjust investment strategies based on real-time data, achieving consistent returns. These examples showcase AI's disruptive impact on the intricacies of the financial landscape.

Ultimately, incorporating AI into finance extends beyond technology, fundamentally reshaping how financial services are delivered and experienced. From safeguarding assets to optimizing individual and portfolio investments, AI empowers institutions and individuals alike, enabling them to navigate the complexities of the financial world with confidence. As AI technologies evolve, the horizon for further innovation appears boundless, offering innumerable opportunities for growth and prosperity within the financial sector.

AI IN CREATIVE INDUSTRIES

In terms of creativity, AI stands as a revolutionary force, providing artists and creators with new avenues to enhance their endeavors. AI challenges norms and fosters new creative avenues from music and art to writing. Consider the realm of music composition: AI tools can now generate harmonious compositions by analyzing numerous musical pieces, detecting patterns, and crafting melodies that resonate with audiences on an emotional level. This capability allows musicians to explore new and uncharted territories of sound, offering fresh perspectives and boundless inspiration. Within visual arts, AI assists artists by analyzing descriptive inputs to generate compelling imagery, transforming abstract concepts into rich visual canvases. Acting like a silent collaborator, AI serves as an artist's assistant, facilitating creative expression that stretches the boundaries of human imagination.

In the evolving landscape of writing, AI further revolutionizes traditional practices. Tools like Grammarly offer real-time spelling, grammar, and style enhancements, ensuring pristine clarity and precision without overshadowing an author's unique voice. Going a step further, advanced AI writing assistants draft content, providing creative frameworks that authors can refine and tailor. This collaboration expedites the writing process and elevates the overall quality of the work produced. Through AI collaboration, writers embark on new stylistic quests, embracing challenges they might have otherwise overlooked—a harmonious partnership where technology and human creativity seamlessly converge to enrich artistic narratives.

AI IN TRANSPORTATION AND LOGISTICS

Within the transportation and logistics industry, AI is driving smarter, more integrated systems that facilitate smoother global movement. Picture a bustling metropolis where traffic flows seamlessly due to AI-regulated traffic management systems. Harnessing real-time data from numerous sources, including cameras and road sensors, these sophisticated systems anticipate traffic disruptions and optimize routes to reduce congestion and minimize travel times for urban dwellers. In logistics, AI commands complex supply chains, projecting demand and optimizing routes for delivery vehicles to ensure punctual deliveries, reduced fuel expenses, and minimized environmental repercussions.

An exciting manifestation of AI innovation is the realm of autonomous vehicles. Autonomous cars deploy sophisticated algorithms to navigate roads with skill, replicating human-like reactions to real-world driving conditions. According to The National Highway Traffic Safety Administration (NTTSA), this AI technology is predicted to reduce accidents caused by human shortcomings by 34%. Logistics enterprises will evolve as autonomous trucks operate without the breaks required for human drivers, reducing operational overheads and optimizing efficiency. Integrating AI into this sector goes beyond simple convenience; it fosters sustainable systems that benefit everyone, including businesses and the public.

AI IN ENVIRONMENTAL CONSERVATION

AI is pivotal in environmental conservation initiatives that affect our planet's well-being. Amidst the challenges of climate change, pioneering solutions are imperative. AI assists in ecological monitoring by dissecting satellite imagery and real-time sensor data, enabling meticulous observation of environmental changes. With exceptional accuracy, researchers track deforestation, wildlife demographics, and land use transformations, identifying patterns early to inform timely conservation interventions and avert potential ecological crises.

AI helps in resource management by forecasting weather and optimizing energy use. It lets wind farms adjust turbines for maximum output and reduced wear. Smart grids use AI to balance supply and demand, minimize waste, and ensure reliable service.

These demonstrations show how AI can be utilized for ecological improvement, providing innovative tools to address some of the most urgent global challenges. Technology integration within conservation strategies signifies a monumental step toward ensuring sustainable resource stewardship, benefiting future generations.

Chapter 10 Reader Quiz

1. True or False: AI-driven fraud detection systems deploy machine learning algorithms to adapt to evolving threat landscapes.
2. True or False: Automated trading algorithms in finance have decreased access to sophisticated trading strategies for individual investors.
3. True or False: AI-powered portfolio optimization tools

employ real-time data analysis to align portfolios with investors' aspirations.

4. True or False: Robo-advisors offer personalized investment advice by examining individual risk profiles.
5. True or False: AI-driven budgeting tools bolster financial transparency by categorizing expenses and providing saving insights.

Answers:

1-True, 2-False, 3-True, 4-True, 5-True

As we close this chapter spotlighting real-world AI success stories, it's clear that AI is paradigm-shifting across sectors, unlocking new prospects and solutions. From amplifying creative fields to refining logistic systems and safeguarding our environment, AI's potential knows no boundaries. In the next chapter, we will explore how AI is already leveraged to create opportunities for development and transformation.

11
MORE ADVANCED AI TOOLS FOR BEGINNERS

"Machine intelligence is the last invention that humanity will ever need to make."

— NICK BOSTROM, AI ETHICS EXPERT IN SWEDEN

EXPLORING ADVANCED INTERACTIONS USING CHATGPT

Imagine navigating a crowded subway with headphones snug in place, not lost in a tune but engaged in a lively conversation with a digital assistant that comprehends you as intimately as a confidant. This is the monumental prowess of ChatGPT, an innovative tool harnessing the power of natural language processing to revolutionize communication. Consider it your 24/7 personal assistant, adeptly managing customer inquiries with elegance. Businesses can harness this prowess to automate FAQs, curating responses that feel warm and genuinely human. Beyond customer service, envision using ChatGPT to weave creative narratives or foster dynamic dialogues. It can architect enthralling stories or facilitate brainstorming sessions, providing an invigorating stimulus to your creative potential.

To illustrate its versatility, imagine a dynamic team meeting conducted entirely via a ChatGPT-supported interface, where team members engage in spontaneous idea exchanges regardless of location. ChatGPT captures notes, suggests agenda items, and proposes next steps, transforming the meeting's efficiency and effectiveness. Another scenario involves educational institutions adopting ChatGPT as a tutor for students, personalizing learning experiences by adapting to each individual's pace and style. The tool can break down complex scientific principles into digestible insights, turning an overwhelming topic into an approachable lesson. These examples accentuate the extensive possibilities of ChatGPT across various contexts.

With proper guidance, using ChatGPT feels as natural as a heartbeat. First, obtain API keys from OpenAI and ensure that all technical prerequisites are met. Tailor prompts to align with your specific tasks, whether it's email drafting or establishing an automated customer support system. Connecting ChatGPT with platforms such as Slack or directly adding it to your website can harmonize interactions, delivering instantaneous assistance to users. This seamless integration elevates the user's experience and boosts operational efficiency. You can tweak ChatGPT's interactions to reflect changes in your business goals by designing specific triggers and responses.

ChatGPT becomes a treasured ally in professional environments, simplifying communication by managing routine inquiries and allowing you to concentrate on more strategic pursuits. ChatGPT works as a virtual editor for writers, aiding in refining text and offering suggestions to enhance clarity and cohesion. Imagine a brainstorming partner that never experiences fatigue and is always ready with fresh perspectives and unique ideas at any hour. This level of support amplifies productivity and stirs creativity, unlocking new vistas in both professional and personal undertakings.

Consider, for instance, an e-commerce platform employing ChatGPT to resolve customer issues, guiding them through product selections, and recommending purchase options based on previous interactions and preferences. A personal touch improves customer satisfaction and helps build long-term brand loyalty. Similarly, creative professionals have embraced ChatGPT in drafting scripts, navigating plot complexities, and unearthing innovative narrative angles. These examples highlight ChatGPT's adaptability and capability to revolutionize interactions across business and creative domains.

Reader Resources: ChatGPT Setup Checklist

- Obtain API keys from OpenAI.
- Customize prompts tailored to specific tasks.
- Seamlessly integrate ChatGPT with messaging platforms.
- Continuously monitor and fine-tune interactions for peak performance.

Armed with these insights, you are ready to explore the full potential that ChatGPT offers.

IDEOGRAM AND CREATIVE AI OUTPUTS

Imagine a realm where your imagination ascends, breaking free from the fetters of traditional tools. Enter Ideogram—a formidable AI force that transmutes abstract notions into breathtaking visuals. This tool transcends mere image creation; it orchestrates a symphony of colors and forms that speak to the artist within all of us. Whether you are envisioning surreal landscapes or developing intricate logos, Ideogram presents a canvas where your dreams gain life through an AI lens. By generating unique visual content, spanning from the fantastical to the hyper-real, Ideogram challenges the boundaries of artistic possibility (SOURCE 3).

Consider the journey of a burgeoning artist who employs Ideogram to experiment with styles reminiscent of the Renaissance period juxtaposed against futuristic digital motifs. He uncovered a new expressive path through this exploration, merging historical inspirations with contemporary technologies. Artists like Quayola exemplify this fusion by reimagining classical masterpieces using digital deconstruction techniques, thus bridging the gap between traditional art forms and modern digital expression. Similarly, museums and art institutions employ AI to connect audiences with art through interactive exhibits.

For instance, the Memphis Museum of Science & History's exhibit "Artificial Intelligence: Your Mind & The Machine" offers visitors hands-on experiences with AI, fostering a dialogue between the audience and the art. These initiatives expand accessibility and engagement with cultural heritage, transforming passive observation into active participation. Ideogram is intuitive and easy to use while being revolutionary in its output.

Commence by crafting prompts that encapsulate the essence of your desired art style or theme. Contemplate the emotion or message you intend to communicate and allow Ideogram to work its magic. The process involves iterating and refining these creations until they resonate with your vision. This cycle of exploration and refinement polishes the final product and enriches your creative journey. With each iteration, you gain insights into your artistic preferences and discover how AI can enhance them. The liberty to experiment is where authentic innovation thrives.

The influence of AI on visual creativity is profound. Artists can venture into previously unfathomable territories by fusing traditional techniques with AI's capabilities. This convergence encourages bold experimentation, nurturing a diversity of visual styles. Envision blending classical painting methods with AI-generated textures; the result is a dynamic interaction between the old and the new, captivating audiences. Ideogram motivates artists to step beyond their comfort zones, fostering a culture of discovery and ingenuity. This union of technology and artistry paves new avenues for expression, challenging our perception of what defines creativity.

Consider the avant-garde artist who curated an exhibit of AI-generated artworks created using Ideogram. Each piece in the exhibit bears witness to an aspect of the relationship between human creativity and AI intelligence. Designers have leveraged Ideogram for concept art in media projects, creating visuals renowned for originality and depth. These examples illuminate how AI-driven art can lead to unexpected and thrilling outcomes, showcasing the boundless possibilities when creativity converges with technology.

Visualize organizing a chaotic workspace, turning disarray into order. Scribbr performs this function for your writing, offering AI-powered suggestions to refine grammar and style, elevating your compositions from draft to polished form. Whether crafting an academic treatise or preparing a professional report, Scribbr ensures integrity with its robust plagiarism detection tools, offering peace of mind regarding originality and credibility (SOURCE 4).

Incorporating Scribbr into your writing workflow is seamless. Establish an account, upload your document, and customize the feedback to satisfy your needs by adjusting style preferences—be it for a formal dissertation or a laid-back blog post. This customization enables Scribbr to deliver personalized insights that augment your writing quality. It is akin to having a seasoned editor available 24 hours a day, proposing suggestions that harmonize with your unique voice.

Further, imagine a university that incorporates Scribbr campus wide as part of its academic resources. Students use it not only for language and stylistic improvements but also to receive feedback on coherence and argument strength, greatly enhancing their learning outcomes. This tool fosters academic integrity by equipping students to recognize and rectify inadvertent plagiarism through its comprehensive checks, promoting originality in scholarly pursuits.

Scribbr excels at maintaining consistency throughout documents, ensuring a coherent voice and style crucial for addressing diverse audiences. By enhancing clarity and readability, Scribbr makes your content accessible to readers with varying expertise levels. It bridges the divide between complex ideas and straightforward communication, ensuring your message connects with clarity.

Envision a student who transformed their essay into a compelling argument using Scribbr's recommendations. The tool guided them in refining their thesis, improving coherence without sacrificing original intent. Similarly, business professionals craft persuasive documents with Scribbr, ensuring every word contributes to the narrative effectively. These examples illustrate Scribbr's role as a catalyst for improved communication, amplifying academic and professional endeavors.

REEDSY: PUBLISHING WITH AI ASSISTANCE

Imagine completing the closing chapter of your manuscript, a labor of love, and now facing the daunting path of self-publishing. Enter Reedsy, a platform that simplifies this process with AI-driven editing and formatting tools, transforming raw text into a market-ready masterpiece. With features optimizing layout and cover design, Reedsy ensures your work reads beautifully and presents professionally. Imagine a virtual editor that hones your prose while a design assistant creates a cover that captures your vision.

To publish with Reedsy, access their user-friendly dashboard and prepare your manuscript according to the guidelines for both digital and print formats. Leverage their marketplace to connect with editors and designers who can further polish your work. This collaborative environment offers industry professionals who are passionate about storytelling. Submit your manuscript through Reedsy's streamlined process for a final transformation into a polished product ready for distribution.

Reflect on a newcomer to the publishing scene, unsure about navigating the industry's complexities. Reedsy equips them with the tools needed to produce a professional-grade book, from the meticulous editing of prose to the attractive aesthetics of cover design, thus democratizing the publishing process. Authors can now concentrate on their creative flow, confident that Reedsy's platform will handle the intricate details with precision and care.

The advantages of AI in publishing are noteworthy. Reedsy's tools enhance editing efficiency, catching errors human eyes might overlook. The formatting tools ensure platform consistency, broadening your book's audience. This precision in editing and design elevates publication quality, providing a competitive edge. With AI assistance, you can focus on creativity while Reedsy manages the technicalities.

Picture authors who've harnessed Reedsy for publishing. One writer, struggling with layout consistency, found Reedsy's tools invaluable, allowing them to focus on narrative instead of formatting dilemmas. Another author collaborated with Reedsy's designers to craft a cover that perfectly represented their book's theme. These success stories highlight how Reedsy empowers authors to bring stories to life with professional finesse and ease.

KEEPING UP WITH AI TRENDS

Navigating the swiftly evolving AI landscape can feel like chasing a fleeting shadow. Yet, this metamorphosis underscores the importance of staying informed. AI's rapid evolution can transform industry standards overnight, expanding boundaries and reshaping practices. Understanding these shifts allows you to fully capitalize on AI's advantages and maintain a lead in your field. New technologies impact everything from business operations to our daily toolsets.

To stay current, subscriptions to AI-focused newsletters or blogs deliver the latest insights directly to your inbox. Research publications and journals offer deep dives into emerging technologies and AI methodologies. Google Alerts for AI topics also help you stay abreast of breakthroughs and trends influencing your sector. This proactive approach ensures you are prepared for fresh AI developments.

In addition, consider attending global AI conferences where premier thinkers and innovators convene to discuss the field's trajectory. Networking with industry peers and participating in workshops at these events offer firsthand glimpses into future advancements. These experiences deepen understanding and prepare you for AI's continuing progression.

AI thought leaders play a pivotal role in knowledge dissemination and perspective shaping. Following influencers on social media offers unique perspectives on trends and new developments. Talks and webinars by pioneers in the AI field offer learning opportunities from the forefront of AI advancement. These experiences are crucial for understanding AI's trajectory.

For deeper exploration, resources like MIT Technology Review and AI Weekly provide starting points with in-depth analyses and broad topic coverage. Podcasts like "The AI Alignment Podcast" and "AI in Business" offer engaging discussions, keeping you informed on your commute or downtime. These platforms inspire critical thinking about AI's societal influence.

Being informed about AI trends isn't just about keeping up; it's about engaging with technology shaping our world. Whether you seek professional competitiveness or are a curious enthusiast, understanding AI's course is imperative.

CONTINUOUS LEARNING AND AI SKILL DEVELOPMENT

In AI's ever-changing realm, lifelong learning is key to staying competitive. The field's rapid evolution demands an adaptable approach. Embracing continuous education exceeds merely keeping pace; it means thriving amid change. New tools and methodologies continuously reshape technological interactions. This evolution requires commitment to ongoing personal and professional growth. Embracing lifelong learning broadens your skill set and unlocks new career opportunities. Consider it a dynamic journey, keeping you engaged and relevant in an ever-shifting landscape.

AI learning resources have become more accessible and convenient than ever. Platforms like Coursera, edX, and Udacity offer a wealth of online courses catering to various skill levels. These platforms equip learners with foundational knowledge and advanced insights, ensuring a comprehensive understanding of AI concepts. For hands-on experience, AI boot camps and workshops offer practical training in real-world scenarios. These immersive experiences bridge theoretical and applicative gaps, equipping you to tackle complex challenges. You can customize your journey with diverse learning options to meet your aspirations.

Structured AI skill development necessitates strategic planning. Start by setting specific, measurable goals aligned with interests and career ambitions. Balance theory with practical application; engage in projects challenging you to apply acquired knowledge. These projects reinforce understanding and build confidence in abilities. By crafting a personalized learning plan, you ensure steady progress and tangible results.

It's about charting a roadmap guiding you through AI complexities, fostering growth at every step.

Certifications and credentials significantly enhance expertise. Formal qualifications validate your skills, boosting industry credibility. You can significantly elevate your career prospects by pursuing certifications like Google's AI certification or enrolling in specialized AI programs from reputable institutions. These credentials reflect your commitment to excellence and signal proficiency to potential employers. In AI's competitive field, recognized qualifications set you apart, providing a solid foundation for future endeavors.

JOIN AI COMMUNITIES FOR SUPPORT

Imagine stepping into a vibrant community where ideas flow freely, backed by unwavering support. Interactions with fellow AI enthusiasts offer spaces for collaboration, insight sharing, and collective growth. The diversity of perspectives enriches understanding, with each member contributing unique experiences and knowledge. This environment fosters innovation, deriving lessons not only from success but also from overcoming challenges. Networking within these circles can lead to professional growth, unveiling opportunities you may not discover alone. Personal engagement in these communities fosters a sense of belonging, like a tribe where your AI passion is comprehended and celebrated.

Participation in these networks is easier than you might think. Online forums like Reddit's Machine Learning community buzz with activity, offering platforms for questions, project sharing, and feedback cultivation. Professional groups like the Association for the Advancement of Artificial Intelligence

(AAAI) provide more formal settings for discourse and development. These spaces are information treasure troves, each thread or discussion offering potential learning. Taking part allows you to consume content and contribute, fostering a dynamic knowledge exchange that benefits everyone involved.

Additionally, virtual meetups and local workshops can connect you to enthusiasts and professionals in your area, strengthening your network through face-to-face interactions and collaborations. These real-world engagements supplement online conversations, building robust professional relationships and community ties in AI development contexts.

Collaboration transforms learning into an interactive experience. Interactions with others reveals alternative perspectives, often leading to innovative solutions. Collaborative projects and hackathons provide fertile grounds for this exchange, pushing boundaries and fueling creativity. Study groups offer peer-to-peer learning structures, making complex concepts approachable through shared efforts. These interactions build skills and confidence, equipping you to tackle challenges independently. Collaboration turns daunting tasks into manageable goals, with each participant contributing to collective success.

Active AI communities like Kaggle significantly enhance learning and collaboration in data science. On Kaggle, members engage in data challenges, sharing strategies and insights that foster a culture of collective problem-solving. This collaborative environment helps participants refine their technical skills and deepens their passion for AI. By joining such networks, individuals become part of a global movement advancing artificial intelligence's frontiers.

Chapter 11 Reader Exercise

Picture crafting a story with minimal input, where AI emerges as your creative partner. Start with a straightforward prompt and observe as AI conjures a narrative with vibrant characters and compelling plots. This exercise transcends mere writing by exploring AI as a co-author. Consider the tone—begin with light-hearted adventures where characters embark on whimsical journeys. Allow AI to fill narrative gaps, weaving a word tapestry that ignites your imagination.

Next, transform the tale into a suspenseful thriller, where shadows lurk and tension mounts with each sentence. This transition challenges you and AI to explore storytelling's dimensions, pushing creativity's boundaries. This exercise lets you grasp AI's flexibility and adaptability, enhancing writing skills and permitting boundless experimentation.

Now try infusing another genre twist, perhaps a science fiction element, requiring AI to build intricate worlds filled with futuristic technologies and cosmic dilemmas. This genre expansion broadens narrative complexity, illustrating AI's capacity to handle diversified themes and plot developments, adding further layers to your storytelling prowess.

These exercises underscore AI's versatility in creative writing, demonstrating its role beyond a mere tool; it extends your imagination. As you engage with these tasks, reflect on how AI can influence writing styles and narrative choices, offering new perspectives and paths previously unexplored.

As this chapter concludes, recognize AI's ability to enhance your creativity and productivity. From writing to the visual arts and beyond, these technologies are accessible to all. Embrace these tools as allies in creative endeavors. In the next chapter, we'll explore AI's industry-shaping power and its impact on sectors like entertainment and healthcare and discuss broader implications for our rapidly evolving world.

12
PERSONALIZED AI JOURNEYS

"The AI does not hate you, nor does it love you, but you are made out of atoms which it can use for something else."

— ELIEZER YUDKOWSKY, CO-FOUNDER OF THE MACHINE INTELLIGENCE RESEARCH INSTITUTE (MIRI)

CRAFTING YOUR UNIQUE AI LEARNING PATH

Imagine stepping into a bustling marketplace where every stall offers opportunities tailored just for you—much like a bespoke suit. This is the essence of designing your personalized AI learning path: a dynamic journey where your choices navigate the expansive landscape of artificial intelligence and find topics that align with your unique interests and career goals.

Whether you are intrigued by the sleek world of machine learning, captivated by the intricate dance of data science, or pondering the philosophical challenges of AI ethics, AI-powered platforms can guide your exploration. For instance, IBM SkillsBuild offers free, customizable courses in AI, data analysis, and cloud computing, enabling learners to earn industry-recognized digital credentials. This platform focuses on underrepresented communities, ensuring more individuals can access quality AI education.

Similarly, DeepLearning.AI, founded by AI pioneer Andrew Ng, provides specialized courses through platforms like Coursera. Their offerings range from foundational topics to advanced subjects like deep learning and neural networks, allowing learners to tailor their educational journey to their interests. By leveraging these resources, you can weave a personalized tapestry of knowledge, merging past inspirations with future technologies and transforming your learning experience into an exciting, tailored adventure.

Identifying personal AI goals requires introspection, an honest conversation with yourself about what fuels your drive. Take time to reflect on what fascinates you about AI. Is it the potential to revolutionize industries, enhance creativity, or solve complex conundrums that draw you in? Perhaps you see AI as a gateway to career advancement or a means to pivot your professional life entirely. Documenting these motivations is not just beneficial—it is essential. Be diligent in drafting these reflections. You might find it helpful to create a vision board or maintain a journal to capture your evolving goals and aspirations; having such visual aids can serve as a persistent reminder of why you set foot on this life-changing path.

Your career ambitions, intertwined with personal interests, will inform your learning journey. Suppose you aim for a data scientist role. In that case, a focus on mastering statistical analysis and machine learning algorithms would be prudent.

Conversely, if your fascination lies with the ethical ramifications of AI, delving into societal impacts and regulatory frameworks might be your course of action. The beauty of AI lies in its versatility—it offers an abundance of potential career paths, whether as an AI ethicist, a machine learning engineer, or even a role in sectors like finance, healthcare, or entertainment. AI serves as a bridge between disciplines, driving innovation beyond traditional limits and enabling collaboration across industries.

A tailored learning approach is the cornerstone of success. Tailoring your educational journey to accommodate your strengths and needs enhances engagement and retention. Unlike traditional education models lounging in a one-size-fits-all approach, personalized learning acknowledges your unique pace and style. You might find enormous value in video tutorials or infographics if you are a visual learner. Conversely, if practical application is your forte, seek out projects, workshops, and hackathons that allow you to apply concepts in real-world scenarios, effectively bridging the occasionally daunting gap between theoretical knowledge and practical application.

Flexibility is a crucial pillar of this journey. As you delve deeper into AI, you may encounter new areas that captivate your imagination. You might start with a concentration on natural language processing, only to uncover an unexpected passion for computer vision or reinforcement learning. Welcome these shifts in interest—they signify a natural evolution of your understanding—and adjust your learning strategy accordingly. This adaptability keeps your curiosity alive and ensures a path aligned with genuine interests, cultivating a richer, more fulfilling educational experience.

Consider the stories of individuals who have successfully tailored their AI learning experiences. Take Maria, for instance, who switched her career trajectory from graphic design to AI. She began by enrolling in online courses focused on data visualization, incorporating these new skills into her existing repertoire. Eventually, she adopted machine learning techniques and transformed her career. Today, Maria heads a creative team using AI to craft dynamic visual content—a testament to how personalized learning can open unexpected professional opportunities and personal achievements.

To create your custom curriculum, identify key AI areas that fascinate you. Whether it's natural language processing, robotics, or AI ethics, the available scope of topics is truly expansive. Balance theoretical knowledge with hands-on projects to solidify your understanding. Online courses provide structured learning materials that accommodate your pace, while workshops offer hands-on experiences, allowing you to apply learned knowledge in practical scenarios and see firsthand the impact of AI solutions to current problems.

Designing your bespoke education plan involves setting clear, focused objectives and defining milestones. Break your ambitions into manageable segments, making mastery of intricate topics like machine learning attainable. Commence with foundational courses, gradually transitioning to complex subjects. Incorporate regular assessments to evaluate your progress, using them as opportunities for reflection and adjustment. Remember, this journey is uniquely yours—there isn't a rigid script to follow, merely a personalized adventure exploring AI's expansive landscape.

PERSONALIZED AI LEARNING TOOLS.

A wealth of tools and resources supports personalized learning in AI. Platforms like Coursera and edX tailor diverse courses that are suitable for varying skill levels and interests. For those seeking community interaction, Kaggle provides a collaborative environment for project sharing and development alongside a vibrant machine learning and data science community. Interaction with these resources enriches your learning experience while expanding your professional network, connecting you with peers and experts worldwide.

Incorporate varied formats into your learning strategy—videos, articles, podcasts—and don't hesitate to explore unconventional resources such as interactive simulations or virtual labs. These diverse formats cater to assorted learning preferences, ensuring sustained and energetic engagement.

As you navigate this journey, maintain an openness to explore unforeseen avenues. The AI field is vast, brimming with countless opportunities for growth and discovery. Embrace the unknown and leverage the chance to expand your skills, broadening your cognitive horizons by continuously integrating new AI frontiers.

This expedition isn't solely about acquiring technical prowess but cultivating a mindset focused on continuous learning and adaptability. AI technologies are constantly advancing, making it essential for you to update your knowledge and skills continuously. Stay inquisitive and remain proactive in your pursuit of new insights and experiences. Celebrate milestones, regardless of their magnitude—whether completing a challenging course or successfully deploying an AI project at work. These achievements invigorate motivation and serve as powerful reminders of your accomplishments and growth trajectory.

While this path is uniquely yours, remember that you are not alone. Seek mentors who offer guidance and insights, sharing wisdom from their journeys. Join communities where exchanging challenges and victories with others who grasp AI's intricacies further enriches your exploratory journey. Experiment with various tools and methodologies in this marketplace of opportunities until you discover the ones that resonate most with you. Your voyage through AI mirrors your aspirations and passions—a narrative of commitment to growth and innovation.

As you continue crafting your personalized AI journey, consider that the ultimate goal of applying AI technology meaningfully in your chosen transcends accumulating purely theoretical knowledge of AI technologies. Whether invigorating creative projects, optimizing business operations, or tackling societal challenges with AI-driven solutions—your journey is laden with potential for impactful change.

Harness personalization's educational power in your learning path to open doors you had never imagined possible. Let it exemplify your dedication and enthusiasm for mastering this dynamic field—a thrilling adventure of exploration, growth, and boundless possibilities.

Chapter 12 User Exercise

Envision waking up each morning invigorated by the prospect of learning, propelled by the excitement of unveiling new layers within AI's vast domain. This exercise will sustain that drive, transforming your curiosity into tangible skills. It isn't merely about absorbing knowledge; it's about engaging with AI in a manner that resonates personally and professionally. The aim is to create lasting learning experiences, ensuring they linger with you long after you have powered down your screen or closed your textbook.

Start by exploring ways AI can integrate into your daily activities, enhancing efficiency and significantly reducing monotony. Consider tasks you regularly perform that could benefit from AI-based automation or improvement. This might be as straightforward as utilizing AI-powered tools to manage your email more effectively or employing machine learning algorithms to refine project management approaches. Identifying these key areas saves time and exponentially boosts productivity. The exercise is about finding creative methodologies to entwine AI into your daily routine, making it a natural and effective workflow extension.

Next, concentrate on a specific project where you can apply your acquired knowledge. Choose something that aligns with your passions, career aspirations, or personal goals. It could be as simple yet meaningful as creating a rudimentary chatbot or as ambitious as analyzing data trends within your industry or field. The key is to select a project that is challenging yet achievable. This hands-on involvement will cement your understanding, empowering you with confidence to tackle more complex problems and projects in the future.

While working on your project, go beyond intangible results—document your progress meticulously. Track what succeeds and what's ineffective and analyze why. Utilize a combination of notes, diagrams, and even voice memos to capture thoughts and ideas as they arise. This documentation is valuable for future reference and provides insights unique to your learning process.

Incorporate feedback loops into your project work. Share your progress and problems with peers, mentors, or supportive networks offering constructive criticism and encouragement. Their external input can provide fresh perspectives and assist in overcoming challenges you might not perceive on your own. Engaging with others in this capacity fosters a robust sense of community and shared learning, further enriching your experience and expanding your analytical horizons.

To deepen understanding, explore related topics that intersect with your current project. If working on a chatbot, delve into natural language processing or the intricacies of user experience design. This exploration broadens your knowledge base and provides contextual understanding of how different AI components coalesce to create harmonious, functioning systems.

As you progress, set incremental goals to maintain motivation and focus. Break down larger tasks into smaller, manageable steps that are achievable within shorter timeframes, making tangible progress attainable. Celebrate each milestone, regardless of its magnitude. These celebrations reinforce your journey's progress and keep the motivational fires burning bright, urging you to continue pushing onward.

To supplement hands-on work, immerse yourself in a diverse array of learning resources, including online courses, video tutorials, podcasts, and articles covering the latest AI developments. By diversifying the materials you engage with, you attain a more rounded perspective and stay current with evolving technologies and methodologies.

Balance intense learning with breaks for introspection. Pausing from the grind offers clarity and insight, enabling a fresh viewpoint on problem-solving. Use this valuable time to evaluate progress and recalibrate strategies. Also, incorporate regular self-assessment into your routine to highlight areas for improvement and identify subjects warranting further study. This practice fosters continuous growth and encourages an objective stance regarding skills and knowledge.

Embrace a growth mindset throughout this exercise. Recognize setbacks as integral pieces of the learning process that provide valuable lessons. Approach challenges with curiosity and resilience, knowing that each obstacle is a growth opportunity. As you conclude this exercise, reflect on the distance you have traveled since commencing your AI exploration. Consider the skills acquired and knowledge gained. Ponder how you can apply these aptitudes contextually or share them with others on a similar AI learning path.

These insights will shed light on how AI technologies actively shape our world. As you continue delving into AI, remember that this journey marks the beginning of an exciting expedition infused with infinite possibilities. Stay curious, engaged, and cherish each moment of this profound learning adventure.

CONCLUSION

As we reach the last pages of our journey into the world of AI, let's take a moment to reflect on the path we've traveled together. We've delved into the intriguing realm of artificial intelligence, exploring its potential to transform mundane tasks into opportunities for efficiency and creativity. From understanding the basics of AI and machine learning to harnessing these technologies for personal productivity, we've tackled a range of topics designed to empower you, regardless of your technical background.

Throughout this book, we've emphasized that AI isn't just for the tech-savvy. It's a versatile tool that anyone can use to simplify their life and work. We explored how AI can automate repetitive tasks, freeing time for activities that truly matter. We also saw how AI can enhance creativity, allowing you to explore new artistic horizons or streamline your writing. Along the way we also discussed ethical considerations of wielding such powerful technology, and potential implications to society if we fail to use AI responsibly.

The key takeaway is that AI is not a distant, complicated technology reserved for the few. It's accessible, practical, and ready to improve your everyday life. Whether you are using AI to manage your calendar, refine your writing, or create stunning visuals, the potential for increased productivity and creativity is immense.

As you close this book, I encourage you to act. You have gained a wealth of knowledge and practical skills over the past chapters. Now it's time to apply them. Start small—perhaps by automating email sorting or experimenting with AI-powered design tools. As you build confidence, explore more complex applications. Remember, AI is a journey, not a destination. Embrace the learning process, and don't be afraid to experiment.

My vision for this book was not only to make AI accessible but also to inspire a sense of curiosity and empowerment. I hope that by demystifying AI, I have shown you how these tools can be allies in your quest for efficiency and creativity. My career in telecommunications and technology has taught me the value of innovation and continuous improvement. I wanted to share this perspective with you, blending practical insights with a supportive, empathetic approach. I also provide a Glossary of AI terms and a list of AI Applications at the end of this book.

For those eager to further their AI knowledge, numerous resources are available. Consider exploring platforms like Coursera and edX for more in-depth courses. Subscribe to newsletters and blogs like MIT Technology Review to stay updated on AI trends. Engage with AI communities online, such as forums and discussion groups, where you can share experiences and learn from others.

Books and podcasts are excellent for deepening your understanding of AI's broader implications. Titles like "Artificial Intelligence: A Guide to Intelligent Systems" by Michael Negnevitsky offer comprehensive insights into AI's technical aspects. Podcasts such as "The AI Alignment Podcast" discuss AI's philosophical and ethical dimensions, providing things to consider as you navigate this evolving landscape.

In closing, thank you for taking this journey with me. Your willingness to explore and learn is commendable. As you continue to explore AI, remember that the most critical element is not the technology but how you choose to use it. Approach AI with an open mind, a sense of responsibility, and a commitment to making the most of its potential.

Together, let's embrace AI as a tool for positive change, personal growth, and meaningful innovation. Whether you are a student, a professional, or an enthusiast, the world of AI is at your fingertips, ready to enhance your life in ways you might not have imagined. Keep learning, keep exploring, and most importantly, keep pushing the boundaries of what's possible. Welcome to a future where technology and humanity work hand in hand.

REFERENCES

- AI Multiple. (2025). 50 ChatGPT Use Cases with Real-Life Examples in 2025. Retrieved from https://research.aimultiple.com/chatgpt-use-cases/
- Alliance Bernstein. (2025). Deploying AI in Investment Applications: Three Case Studies. Retrieved from https://www.alliancebernstein.com/us/en-us/investments/insights/investment-insights/deploying-ai-in-investment-applications-three-case-studies.html
- Ambit software. (2025). Smarter Insights with Power BI, Tableau & Generative AI. Retrieved from https://ambitsoftware.com/ai-powered-analytics-harnessing-powerbi-tableau-and-generative-ai-for-smarter-insights/
- Atlassian. (2025). AI for Project Management: Tools and Best Practices - Atlassian. Retrieved from https://www.atlassian.com/work-management/project-management/ai-project-management#:~:text=Task%20and%20time%20management&text=AI%20tools%20can%20manage%20tasks%20before%20they%20disrupt%20project%20progress
- Atlassian. (2025). Responsible AI: Key Principles and Best Practices. Retrieved from https://www.atlassian.com/blog/artificial-intelligence/responsible-ai
- AWS. (2025). Exploring Practical Use Cases for Generative AI in Small .... Retrieved from https://aws.amazon.com/blogs/smb/exploring-practical-use-cases-for-generative-ai-in-small-businesses/
- Bitecool. (2025). How to Optimize Your AI Laptop for Maximum Performance in .... Retrieved from https://bitecool.com/blogs/blog/how-to-optimize-your-laptop-for-maximum-performance-in-2024
- Bit Insight Group. AI for SMBs: The Power of Game-Changing IT Services. https://bitinsightgroup.com/the-power-of-ai-for-smbs/
- Blog. (2025). History of AI - first chapter: from Turing to McCarthy - Pigro. Retrieved from https://blog.pigro.ai/en/history-of-artificial-intelligence
- Blog. (2025). How and Where to Integrate ChatGPT on Your Website. Retrieved from https://blog.hubspot.com/website/chatgpt-integration

- Calmu. (2025). 16 Artificial Intelligence Career Paths. Retrieved from https://www.calmu.edu/news/artificial-intelligence-career-paths
- Chisw. (2025). The Future of AI in Retail: Trends with Case Studies. Retrieved from https://chisw.com/blog/ai-in-retail-trends-future/
- Developers. (2025). Machine Learning Crash Course. Retrieved from https://developers.google.com/machine-learning/crash-course
- Digitalocean. (2025). 10 AI Music Generators for Creators in 2025. Retrieved from https://www.digitalocean.com/resources/articles/ai-music-generators
- Prasad, R. K. (2024, June 18). *Understanding AI: Overcoming fear and embracing the future*. eLearning Industry. https://elearningindustry.com/understanding-ai-overcoming-fear-and-embracing-the-futureeLearning Industry
- Filimowicz, M. (n.d.). *The history and evolution of AI-generated art*. Medium. https://medium.com/higher-neurons/the-history-and-evolution-of-ai-generated-art-e5ccca5a8e83
- Ideogram. (2025). Welcome to Ideogram | Ideogram. Retrieved from https://docs.ideogram.ai/#:~:text= Ideogram%20(pronounced%20%22eye%2Ddee%20im-ages%2C%20innovative%20logos%20and%20posters.
- Forbes. (2025). Personalized Learning And AI: Revolutionizing Education. Retrieved from https://www.forbes.com/councils/forbestechcouncil/2024/07/22/personalized-learning-and-ai-revolutionizing-education/
- G2. (2025). Top 10 Otter.ai Alternatives & Competitors in 2025. Retrieved from https://www.g2.com/products/otter-ai/competitors/alternatives
- Getclockwise. (2025). Time Management with AI: Tools & Tips. Retrieved from https://www.getclockwise.com/blog/ai-time-management
- Grow.Google. (2025). AI courses and tools from Google. Retrieved from https://grow.google/ai/
- IBM. (2025). Exploring privacy issues in the age of AI. Retrieved from https://www.ibm.com/think/insights/ai-privacy
- Innopharmaeducation. (2025). The Impact of AI on Job Roles, Workforce, and Employment. Retrieved from https://www.innopharmaeducation.com/blog/the-impact-of-ai-on-job-roles-workforce-and-employment-what-you-need-to-know
- Intellias. (2025). AI in Decision Making: What Is It, Benefits & Examples. Retrieved from https://intellias.com/ai-decision-making/

- Itransition.com. (n.d.). *AI in Education: 8 Use Cases & Real-Life Examples.* Retrieved from https://www.itransition.com/ai/education
- Kaggle. (2025). Kaggle: Your Machine Learning and Data Science Community. Retrieved from https://www.kaggle.com/
- Kolabtree. (2021, July 29). *AI in Healthcare: 5 Real-World Examples.* News-Medical. https://www.news-medical.net/whitepaper/20181107/AI-in-Healthcare-5-Real-World-Examples.aspx
- Languagemagazine. (2025). Using AI to Save Time and Lessen the Load. Retrieved from https://languagemagazine.com/2024/09/19/using-ai-to-save-time-and-lessen-the-load/
- Kisling, Nestico & Redick. (n.d.). *Self-driving car accident statistics.* KNR Legal. https://www.knrlegal.com/car-accident-lawyer/self-driving-car-accident-statistics/**:contentReference[oaicite:1]{index=1}
- Mentimeter. (2025). Free AI Quiz Generator: Create Quizzes with AI. Retrieved from https://www.mentimeter.com/features/ai-quiz-generator
- Martínez Hernández, J. (2024). Performance of API Design for Interoperability of Medical Information Systems. Applied Sciences, 14(9), 3944.
- Microsoft. (2025). How to Set Realistic Goals with AI—Microsoft 365. Retrieved from https://www.microsoft.com/en-us/microsoft-365-life-hacks/organization/set-goals-with-ai
- MSRcosmos. (n.d.). AI in the Retail Industry (Use Cases & Real-World Examples). https://www.msrcosmos.com/uses-cases/ai-in-the-retail-industry-use-cases-real-world-examples/
- OpenAI. (2025). Dall-E 2. Retrieved from https://openai.com/index/dall-e-2/
- Reid, S. G. (n.d.). *Dissecting algorithmic trading.* Turing Finance. https://www.turingfinance.com/dissecting-algorithmic-trading/
- Restack. (2025). Top Beginner-Friendly AI Tools 2023 | Restack.io. Retrieved from https://www.restack.io/p/beginner-friendly-ai-answer-top-tools-github-2023-cat-ai
- ScienceDirect. (2025). A systematic review of AI education in K-12 classrooms .... Retrieved from https://www.sciencedirect.com/science/article/pii/S2666920X24000122
- Scimedian. (2025). 10 Case Studies of Successful Implementation of AI in .... Retrieved from https://scimedian.in/10-case-studies-of-successful-implementation-of-ai-in-healthcare/

- Scribbr. (2025). AI Proofreader | Your Paper Corrected in Minutes. Retrieved from https://www.scribbr.com/ai-proofreader/
- Sembly. (2025). Using AI in Project Management: Key Tools and Benefits. Retrieved from https://www.sembly.ai/blog/ai-in-project-management-key-tools-and-benefits/
- Tableau. (2025). Everyday examples and applications of artificial .... Retrieved from https://www.tableau.com/data-insights/ai/examples
- TechTarget. (2025). The History of Artificial Intelligence: Complete AI Timeline. Retrieved from https://www.techtarget.com/searchenterpriseai/tip/The-history-of-artificial-intelligence-Complete-AI-timeline
- The Guardian. (2024, December 6). How AI monitoring is cutting stillbirths and neonatal deaths in a clinic in Malawi. https://www.theguardian.com/global-development/2024/dec/06/how-ai-monitoring-is-cutting-stillbirths-and-neonatal-deaths-in-a-clinic-in-malawi
- Timetracko. Artificial Intelligence and Machine Learning in Radiology. https://timetracko.com/blog/artificial-intelligence-and-machine-learning-in-radiology/
- Toolify. (2025). Canva AI vs. Mid-Journey: A Comparison of Design .... Retrieved from https://www.toolify.ai/ai-news/canva-ai-vs-midjourney-a-comparison-of-design-generation-tools-2500624
- Toools. (2025). Best AI Tools for Designers & Marketers. Retrieved from https://www.toools.design/ai-tools-for-designers-and-marketing
- UNESCO. (2025). Ethics of Artificial Intelligence. Retrieved from https://www.unesco.org/en/artificial-intelligence/recommendation-ethics
- University of Iowa. (2025). The Role of AI in Modern Education. Retrieved from https://onlineprograms.education.uiowa.edu/blog/role-of-ai-in-modern-education
- Usemotion. (2025). We Tested 50+ AI Productivity Tools. Here Are The 16 Best .... Retrieved from https://www.usemotion.com/blog/ai-productivity-tools
- Usemotion. (2025). We Tested 50+ AI Productivity Tools. Here Are The 16 Best .... Retrieved from https://www.usemotion.com/blog/ai-productivity-tools
- Vasconcelos, M. A. R., & dos Santos, R. P. (2023). *Enhancing STEM learning with ChatGPT and Bing Chat as objects to think with: A case study*. arXiv. https://doi.org/10.48550/arXiv.2305.02202

- Vinay Kumar Moluguri. (2025). Google's Teachable Machine AI: Step-By-Step Tutorial Included. Retrieved from https://vinaykumarmoluguri.medium.com/googles-teachable-machine-ai-step-by-step-tutorial-included-6a7200199932
- Yahoo Finance. (2025). 15 Best AI Tools for Education in 2023 - Yahoo Finance. Retrieved from https://finance.yahoo.com/news/15-best-ai-tools-education-052148514.html
- Yahoo Finance. (2025). How to use AI to improve your finances. Retrieved from https://finance.yahoo.com/personal-finance/banking/article/ai-for-finance-145409227.html
- Yomu.ai. (2025). Grammarly vs. AI Writing Assistants: Which One is Better for .... Retrieved from https://www.yomu.ai/resources/grammarly-vs-ai-writing-assistants-which-one-is-better-for-writers
- Zapier. (2025). Evernote Trello Integration - Quick Connect. Retrieved from https://zapier.com/apps/evernote/integrations/trello
- Zapier. (2025). The seven best AI email assistants. Retrieved from https://zapier.com/blog/best-ai-email-assistant/
- Zapier. (2025). The eight best AI scheduling assistants. Retrieved from https://zapier.com/blog/best-ai-scheduling/
- Zapier. (2025). The eight best AI tools for social media management in 2025. Retrieved from https://zapier.com/blog/best-ai-social-media-management/

GLOSSARY OF AI TERMS

- **AI**—Short for Artificial Intelligence, is the field of computer science focused on building intelligent machines that can think, learn, and solve problems in the same manner as humans.
- **API**—Short for Application Programming Interface, a tool that allows different software applications to communicate with each other.
- **Artificial Neural Network**—A computing system inspired by the human brain's structure, used in deep learning.
- **Augmented Reality**—A technology that overlays digital information onto the real world, often enhanced with AI.
- **Automation**—Using technology to perform tasks automatically without human intervention.
- **Bias**—A tendency of an AI system to make errors or skew results due to flawed training data or assumptions.
- **Cloud Computing**—Storing and accessing data and programs over the internet instead of a local computer.
- **Computer Vision**—An area of AI that enables machines to interpret and make decisions based on visual data.
- **Data Mining**—The process of analyzing large datasets to find useful patterns or information.
- **Data Privacy**—Protecting personal and sensitive information from unauthorized access or misuse.
- **Data Science**—The study of data using statistics, machine learning, and visualization to derive insights and inform decisions.
- **Deep Learning**—An advanced form of machine learning using neural networks to handle complex problems like image or voice recognition.
- **Digital Twin**—A virtual model that simulates the behavior of a physical object or system.
- **edX**—An online learning platform with courses in AI and other fields from global universities.
- **Ethical AI**—The development and deployment of AI systems that align with ethical principles such as fairness and transparency.

- **GPT-3 - A** powerful language model developed by OpenAI that can write and converse like a human.
- **Generative AI**—AI that can create new content, such as images, text, or music, often using existing data as a reference.
- **Inference**—The process of making predictions using a trained AI model.
- **Kaggle**—A platform for data science competitions and AI learning projects.
- **LLM**—Short for Large Language Model, an advanced AI model trained on vast amounts of text to understand and generate language.
- **ML**—An abbreviation for Machine Learning.
- **Machine Learning**—A type of AI that enables computers to learn from data and improve their performance without being explicitly programmed.
- **Model**—A mathematical representation of a real-world process used by AI to analyze and interpret data.
- **Open Source**—Software with publicly available code that anyone can use, modify, and share.
- **OpenAI**—An AI research and deployment company known for creating tools like ChatGPT and DALL-E.
- **Overfitting**—A modeling error where an AI system performs well on training data but poorly on new, unseen data.
- **Predictive Modeling**—Using historical data and statistical techniques to forecast future outcomes.
- **Prompt Engineering**—The practice of crafting effective input statements to get desired responses from AI models.
- **Reinforcement Learning**—A type of machine learning where systems learn by trial and error, receiving rewards or penalties for actions.
- **Speech Recognition**—The ability of a machine to identify and process spoken language into text.
- **TensorFlow**—An open-source platform for building and training AI and machine learning models.
- **Training Data**—The data used to teach an AI model how to make predictions or decisions.
- **Turing Test**—A test developed by Alan Turing to determine whether a machine can exhibit intelligent behavior indistinguishable from a human.

- **Underfitting**—A problem where a model is too simple to capture the patterns in the data effectively.
- **Virtual Assistant**—An AI software agent that helps users perform tasks or services, such as scheduling or research.
- **Voice Assistant**—An AI-powered application like Siri or Alexa that understands and responds to voice commands.

AI TOOLS REFERENCED IN THIS BOOK

AnyList—A smart grocery list and recipe app that can suggest items and organize shopping.
https://www.anylist.com
Asana—A task management platform that helps teams organize and track work projects.
https://asana.com
Atticus—A tool that helps authors format and publish books easily and professionally.
https://atticus.io
Buffer - A social media scheduling tool for planning, publishing, and monitoring social media posts.
https://buffer.com
Calendly—An AI-based scheduling assistant that automates meeting bookings.
https://calendly.com
Canva—A graphic design platform used to create social media graphics and presentations.
https://www.canva.com
ChatGPT—An AI chatbot developed by OpenAI that can write and answer questions like a human.
https://chat.openai.com
Clean Email—An AI tool that organizes and declutters your inbox automatically.
https://clean.email
ClickUp—An all-in-one productivity platform for tasks, docs, goals, and project management.
https://www.clickup.com
Clockwise - A smart calendar assistant that optimizes your schedule based on your work habits.
https://www.getclockwise.com
Coursera—An online learning platform with AI and technology courses from top universities.
https://www.coursera.org
DALL-E—An AI image generator by OpenAI that creates pictures from text prompts.
https://openai.com/dall-e
DIY Book Covers—An online tool to create 3D and 2D book cover mockups for marketing.

https://diybookcovers.com

Evernote - note taking and organization app for managing tasks, documents, and ideas.

https://evernote.com

Hootsuite - A social media scheduling tool for planning, publishing, and monitoring social media posts of large enterprises.

https://www.hootsuite.com/

Google Calendar—A calendar tool that integrates with AI for smart scheduling and reminders.

https://calendar.google.com

Google Photos—A photo storage tool that uses AI to organize and recognize images.

https://photos.google.com

Grammarly—A writing assistant that corrects grammar and enhances clarity using AI.

https://www.grammarly.com

Hootsuite - A comprehensive social media management and automation platform.

https://hootsuite.com

Ideogram—An AI-powered tool that generates images from text prompts.

https://ideogram.ai

Kaggle—A platform for data science competitions and learning AI with real datasets.

https://www.kaggle.com

Midjourney—An AI art generator that creates images from descriptive text prompts.

https://www.midjourney.com

Mint—A personal finance app that tracks spending and creates budgets.

Mint: https://mint.intuit.com

Monday.com—A work operating system that uses AI to automate project management.

https://monday.com

Notion—An AI-enhanced workspace for notes, tasks, databases, and collaboration.

https://www.notion.so

OpenAI—The company that developed ChatGPT, DALL-E, and other AI tools.

https://openai.com

Otter - An AI-powered transcription tool for meetings, interviews, and lectures.

Otter: https://otter.ai

Reedsy—A book editing and formatting tool tailored for self-publishing authors.

https://reedsy.com

RescueTime—A time-tracking app that uses AI to show how you spend your day.
https://www.rescuetime.com
SaneBox—An AI-powered tool that filters unimportant emails from your inbox.
https://www.sanebox.com
Scribbr—A citation and grammar checker for academic writing powered by AI.
https://www.scribbr.com
TensorFlow—An open-source platform used to build and train machine learning models.
https://www.tensorflow.org
Todoist - A Task manager that uses AI to help prioritize and organize to-dos.
https://todoist.com
Trello—A visual project management app that helps track tasks and workflows.
https://trello.com
YNAB—A budgeting tool that uses automation to help you plan and manage personal finances.
https://www.youneedabudget.com
edX—An online learning platform offering free and paid courses in AI and more.
https://www.edx.org
x.ai—An AI-powered personal assistant that helps schedule meetings via email.
https://x.ai

www.ingramcontent.com/pod-product-compliance
Lightning Source LLC
LaVergne TN
LVHW100315210926
848480LV00003B/1137